The Voice of
The Beloved

The Voice of
The Beloved

by: Viola Yassa

ST SHENOUDA PRESS
SYDNEY, AUSTRALIA
2021

The Voice of the Bleloved

COPYRIGHT © 2021
St Shenouda Press

All rights reserved. Except for brief quotations in critical publications or reviews, no part of this book may be reproduced in any manner without prior written permission from the publisher.

ST SHENOUDA PRESS
8419 Putty Rd,
Putty, NSW, 2330
Australia

www.stshenoudapress.com

ISBN 13: 978-0-6451394-8-8

CONTENTS

INTRODUCTION	7
HIS VOICE IN LIFE AND BEYOND	11
WAYS GOD REVEALS HIMSELF	27
HISTORY OF SALVATION IN THE BIBLE	59
DO WE HEAR GOD'S VOICE?	71
ALIVE OR DEAD	93
JESUS RAISES AND JUDGES	117
TWO RESURRECTIONS	133
THE FIRST RESURRECTION	137
THE ONE THOUSAND-YEAR REIGN	184
THE RESURRECTION OF THE DEAD	215
WE GROAN IN HOPE	235

INTRODUCTION

The very God of the universe speaks on every page of the Holy Bible into my mind — and your mind. We hear His Very Words. God Himself has multiplied His wondrous deeds and thoughts toward us; none can compare with Him! I will proclaim and tell of them, yet they are more than can be told (Ps40:5).

And best of all, they are available to all. O, how precious is the Bible. It is the very Word of God. In it God speaks in the twenty-first century. This is the very voice of God. By this voice, He speaks with absolute truth and personal force. By this voice, he reveals His all-surpassing beauty. By this voice, He reveals the deepest secrets of our hearts. No voice anywhere anytime can reach as deep or lift as high or carry as far as the voice of God that we hear in the Bible.

We can have confidence that we will hear His voice. The Apostle Paul writes in Rom8:14, "For as many as are led by the Spirit of God, these are sons of God." Conversely, this scripture implies that if we are God's children, if we are baptised (born-again), we will be led by His Spirit. We have further assurance of this promise in Ps37:23-24, "The steps of a good (righteous, born-again) person are ordered by the Lord, and He delights in his way. Though he falls, he shall not be utterly cast down; for the Lord upholds him with His hand." God will order our steps, and even when we blow it, if we are truly trying to do His will, He will lift us up and give us a second chance.

The great need of our time is for people to experience the living reality of God by hearing His Word personally and His transforming power in Scripture. The most difficult part of hearing God is the fact that it takes time to learn to discern God's voice, and it takes a humble heart. Jer29:12-13 says, "Then you will call upon Me and go and pray to Me, and I will listen to you. And you will seek Me and find Me, when you search for Me with all your heart." We can't make demands on Almighty God. We can't shake our fist at the sky and say, 'all right God, let me hear you.' But we can ask, seek, and knock, and the Bible promises that God will open the door. God will reveal Himself to those who humbly seek Him. "Trust in the Lord with all your heart, and lean not on your own understanding; in all your ways acknowledge Him, And He shall direct your paths," Pr3:5-6.

In fact, there are three voices that we can hear: the voice of God, the voice of our own fleshly desires, and the voice of the Devil. However, we can train our ear to recognize the voice of God above all the noise. It is by practicing, by reason of use, that we are able to discern whether what we hear is of God, our flesh, or the Devil.

Something is incredibly wrong when the words we hear outside Scripture are more powerful and more affecting to us than the inspired Word of God. Let us cry with the psalmist, "Incline my heart to your Word," Ps119:36. "Open my eyes, that I may behold wondrous things out of Your Law," Ps119:18. Grant that the eyes of our hearts would be enlightened to know our hope and our inheritance and the love of Christ that passes knowledge and be filled with all the fullness of God (Eph1:18; 3:19).

HIS VOICE IN LIFE AND BEYOND

"God, who at various times and in various ways spoke in time past to the fathers by the prophets, has in these last days spoken to us by His Son, whom He has appointed heir of all things, through whom also He made the worlds," Heb1:1-2.

What these two verses teach very loudly and plainly is that God is not silent. God is not withdrawn and uncommunicative. He means to connect with us. He is not an idea to be thought about. He is a person to be listened to and understood and enjoyed and obeyed. He is a speaking Person. There is no more important fact than this: There is a God who speaks that we might know Him and love Him and live in joyful obedience to Him. God spoke.

They also teach us that God has spoken in two phases: before the coming of the Son of God into the world and through the Son of God's coming into the world. This indicates that God's Communication now is better and greater than before. God exists, and He speaks to man. Consider these two phases of God's communication for a moment.

GOD SPOKE IN THE PROPHETS

Before the coming of the Son it says God spoke "in the prophets" in many portions (or many times or many places) and in many ways. When God spoke to the fathers in the prophets, God spoke to the fathers! When the fathers heard and understood the prophets, they heard God speaking. God uses chosen, inspired human instruments to speak to the fathers. But it is God speaking to the fathers when the prophets speak and write.

God spoke "in the Prophets" or by the Prophets means that God's typical way of communicating with His people as a whole was by inspiring human spokesmen as go-betweens. It was not God's way to write His Word in the sky, or to shout it from mountains for all to hear, or to whisper it one by one in the heart of every Israelite. His usual way was to call a prophet and then inspire the prophet to speak and to write to the people what God wanted said.

The revelation given through the prophets was brought in various ways - sometimes through parables, historical narrative, prophetic confrontation, dramatic presentation, psalms, proverbs, and the like.

Old Testament Scriptures document that God spoke long ago:

God spoke to Adam and told him that the Saviour would come from the Seed of the woman (Gn3:15).

God spoke to Abraham and told him that the Saviour would come from his Seed (Gn12:3, 18:18, 22:18).

God spoke to Jacob and told him that the Saviour would come through the tribe of Judah (Gn49:10).

God spoke to David and told him that the Saviour would be born of his house (2Sam7:16).

God spoke to Micah and told him that the Saviour would be born at Bethlehem (Mic5:2).

God spoke to Isaiah and told him that the Saviour would be born of a virgin (Is7:14).

Thus, the prophets were the mouthpieces of God and their words were not the production of their own spirit, but came from the Holy Spirit as emphasized by St Peter who wrote that "no prophecy was ever made by an act of human will, but men moved by the Holy Spirit spoke from God," 1Pt1:21.

The prophet John the Baptist quotes another prophet, Isaiah, explaining that he was but "a voice of One who is crying out in the wilderness" (Jn1:23); the One giving the message was God, John being His voice, "a vessel for honour, sanctified, useful to the Master, prepared for every good work" (2Ti2:21).

The prophets received their call or appointment directly from God, and some like Jeremiah (Jer1:5) or John the Baptist (Jn1:13, 14, 15), were called before birth. Although not all that God had spoken through the prophets was predictive prophecy, this aspect of God's revelation is one of the strongest evidences that the Bible is divinely inspired.

The speech of God throughout the ages past was not unbroken chatter but given in episodes of speech punctuating seasons of silence (e.g. 400 silent years of the inter-testament period). This phrase is first in the Greek construction for emphasis and refers to the incremental and progressive revelation (Genesis gives some truth, Exodus some more truth, etc.) in which God disclosed Himself in portions of truth at different times until the appearance of the Son, Who Himself is the consummation of Truth (Jn1:17, Jn14:6), the fulfilment of the Law and Prophets (Mt5:17).

The prophetic revelation was fragmentary, piece by piece in 49 Old Testament books delivered over some 1500 years by more than forty writers, each contributing "portions" of divine revelation, none in themselves complete. Finally, the revelation is complete in Christ. Hallelujah!

In "many ways" points to the different media and modes through which God disclosed His word, including dream, direct voice, signs, angelic visitations and even in different ways to different men. He spoke to Moses in the burning bush (Ex3:2), to Elijah in a still, small voice (1Kg19:12), to Isaiah in a vision in the temple (Is6:1), to Hosea in his family circumstances (Hos1:2), and to Amos in a basket of summer fruit (Am8:1).

"Many ways" also allude to the different Old Testament literary types including law, history, poetry, allegory, prophecy, etc. St Paul's main point in this section is to emphasize that all Old Testament revelation was God speaking to man, although in a manner that was fragmentary and occasional, lacking fullness and finality.

The Gospel revelation is excellent above the former; in that it is a revelation which God has made by His Son. In beholding the power, wisdom, and goodness of the Lord Jesus Christ, we behold the power, wisdom, and goodness of the Father, Jn14:7; the fullness of the Godhead dwells, not typically, or in a figure, but really, in Him. When, on the fall of man, the world was breaking to pieces under the curse of God, the Son of God, undertaking the work of redemption, sustained it by His almighty power and goodness. From the glory of the person and office of Christ, we proceed to the glory of His Grace.

We never can be thankful enough that God has in so many ways, and with such increasing clearness, spoken to us fallen sinners concerning salvation. That He should by Himself cleanse us from our sins is a wonder of love beyond our utmost powers of admiration, gratitude, and praise.

GOD SPOKE TO US BY HIS SON

"In these last days (God) has spoken to us in His Son," Heb1:2. Now the point here is that if God seemed ready and eager to communicate Himself in the Old Testament, how much more is He ready to communicate in the sending of His Son! What St Paul wants us to see is that this latest communication from God is greater and better than all those portions and ways in days of old. So, when I complain to God, "Lord, I want to hear You. Would You speak to me? I need to hear Your voice . . .", is my complaint well placed? What would God's response be in view of these words? Let's look at three ways that the speaking of God in the Son in these last days is better than God's speaking of old.

First, God has now spoken not just by prophets, but by His Son. "God, after He spoke long ago to the fathers in the prophets in many portions and in many ways, in these last days has spoken to us in His Son." Notice it does not say, "Formerly God spoke by prophets and in these last days He has spoken by apostles." That's true. And you can see their crucial role in Heb2:3-4. But the point here is that in these last days God has done something very different: to communicate, He sent His Son.

Again, God, after He spoke long ago to the fathers in the prophets in many portions and in many ways, in these last days has spoken to us in His Son. This is different. The Son of God is not just a prophet. Some thought He was just a prophet (Jn9:17), but He was not a mere prophet. Here Islam makes a great mistake about Jesus. Jesus is not only a prophet like Moses or Isaiah. And He is far above Mohammed in glory. He is the Son of God. And that means He is God. The son of Adam is human like Adam. And the Son of God is divine like God.

"He is the radiance of (God's) glory and the exact representation of (God's) nature," Heb1:2. The point of those words is to warn us against the mistake that Islam has made. Jesus is the unique image of God's divine glory and bears the very stamp of His divine nature. He is not a mere prophet. The whole point here is to show that He is superior to the prophets. He is the Eternally Begotten Son, without beginning and without ending (Heb7:3).

In other words, God has not just spoken by inspiring prophets and apostles. He has spoken by coming to us in the person of His Son. Who Jesus was, what He said, and what He accomplished by dying and rising from the dead is God's Word to us. This is what God has said, and what we should hear — what we need to listen to far more earnestly than we do.

Have I Heard the Word of God in the Person of Jesus? Every time I begin to complain that God is silent and that I need God to speak to me — at that moment I should stop and ask: Have I heard this Word? Is this Word from God — spoken in the Son of God — so short and simple that I have finished with it, and now I need more — another word? Have I really heard the Word of God in the person and the teaching and the work of the Son? Is the aching of my soul and the confusion of my mind really owing to the fact that I have exhausted hearing this Word and need another word? And so, I feel another gracious rebuke to my unperceptive and presumptuous ears.

So, the first way that the speaking of God is better in these last days than in the prophets of old is that He has now spoken in the coming of His Son.

The second way that the speaking of God in these last days is better than in the former days is that the Son in whom He speaks has been appointed heir of all things. "In these last days (God) has spoken to us in His Son, whom He appointed heir of all things," Heb1:2. Now why does St Paul add this? Because he wants us to dwell on the fact that the one we listen to, Jesus, the Son of God, can make good in the end on all that He promises. Why? Because He is the heir of all things. In the end, He will have at His disposal all things. He will have in subjection to Him all that is. He can make good on all his promises. If he says, "Blessed are the meek for they shall inherit the earth," (Mt5:5), then He can make good on that promise, because He will own the earth and have it under His control. If He says, "Nothing in all creation will separate us from the love of God in Christ Jesus" (Rom8:39), then He can make good on that promise because He will own all creation and have it under His control. If He says, "There shall no longer be death or mourning or crying or pain any more" (Rev21:1), He can make good on that promise because He will own life and death and rule unhindered over all that causes pain and crying.

 *When you listen to the Son of God, it is different from listening to a prophet. God will make good on the word of the prophets. But the Son will make good on His Own Word*

I wonder if you have ever asked why the Son in Heb1:2 is described first as the "heir of all things" and second as the one "through whom God made the world?" Why not say first that He is Creator of all things, and second that He is Heir of all things? What is ultimately at stake in my life (and your life) is how the future goes, not how the past went. If I have a Saviour who is heir of all things and makes everything serve my everlasting joy, then the past is important only to the degree that it helps me understand that and believe that and live in the truth of that. But it's the future where I will live — or not.

But the fact is, we cannot understand Jesus' being appointed Heir of all things until we understand that all things were made through Him. Until you know this, you might say, 'Oh, Jesus was a man like us and was chosen to be exalted to some special role as heir — after all it says, he was "appointed" heir! So, if he was "appointed" heir, then maybe he was not always heir and he was really adopted as a Son of God rather than being the Son of God eternally.' That would be a huge mistake.

So, St Paul follows his first and primary statement that the Son is "the heir of all things" with the statement that "through him God made the world." This means at least two things:

- The Son existed before He came to earth in the person of Jesus of Nazareth;

- The Son already owned the universe by virtue of creating it with the Father. In fact, Heb1:3 says, "He upholds all things by the word of His power." (See also Heb1:10-12.)

So, He created all and He upholds all. How then is He "appointed" heir of all? For now, much of His creation is in rebellion against Him; and God has ordained that, because of the Son's faithful obedience and death and resurrection, these enemies will one day be subdued and all creation will bow down and acknowledge that they are ruled and owned by Jesus Christ.

"Having offered one sacrifice for sins for all time, (Christ) sat down at the right hand of God, waiting from that time onward until his enemies be made a footstool for his feet," Heb10:1-13.

In other words, Christ took His seat as the active ruling heir of all things by virtue of His death and resurrection (Heb10:12-13). He not only has the right to be the heir of all things because He made all things, but also because He defeated His enemies and purchased a lost people from sin and death through His death.

So, we have double reason to give heed to a Son of God who is heir of all things: He is heir in one sense because He made all things; and He is appointed heir in another sense because He died and rose again to redeem for Himself a people and to destroy Sin and death and Satan and everything that could make His people miserable.

He can make good on His word because He is God, because He is Creator, and because He is the Triumphant Heir over all evil and misery. This is a better word than anything the prophets ever spoke in many ways in the Old Testament.

The third reason about how superior God's speaking in the Son is over His speaking of old in the prophets is that this Word of God in His son is so decisive and so full that there will be no third phase of God's speaking in history. That is what it means when it says in Heb1:2: "in these last days (God) has spoken to us in His Son." The last days begin with the coming of the Son into the world. We have been living in the last days since the days of Christ — that is, the last days of history as we know it before the final and full establishment of the Kingdom of God.

The last days of a war are the days after the decisive battle has been fought or the decisive bomb has been dropped. Everyone knows who will win. It is only a matter of time. The resistance may go on for some years, but the mortal blow has been struck to the enemy and the high ground has been captured. The days of fighting that remain are the last days of the war.

So, it is since the Son of God came into the world. In His death and resurrection, the decisive battle with Sin and death and hell has been fought and won. It is only a matter of time. These are the last days bringing His decisive triumph to all the peoples of the earth. The Word that God spoke by His Son is the decisive Word. It will not be followed in this age by any greater word or replacement word. This is the Word of God — the person of Jesus, the teaching of Jesus, and the work of Jesus.

When I complain that I don't hear the Word of God, when I feel a desire to hear the voice of God, and get frustrated that He does not speak in ways that I may crave, what am I really saying? Am I really saying that I have exhausted this final decisive Word revealed to me so fully in the New Testament? Have I really exhausted this Word? Has it become so much a part of me that it has shaped my very being and given me life and guidance? Or have I treated it lightly — skimmed it like a newspaper, dipped in like a taste tester — and then decided I wanted something different, something more? This is what I fear I am guilty of more than I wish to admit.

WAYS GOD REVEALS HIMSELF

The Bible says that God has revealed Himself to humanity in four different ways. They include:

1. Nature
2. Our Conscience
3. Jesus Christ
4. The Bible

NATURE HAS REVEALED GOD

The universe with its vastness and complexity gives testimony to God and His glory. The Bible says: "When I consider your heavens, the work of your fingers, the moon and the stars, which you have ordained, what is man that you are mindful of him," Ps8:3,4.

Yet the testimony of nature only tells us about God in a limited way. The Book of Job states this fact. "He binds up the water in His thick clouds, yet the clouds are not broken under it. He covers the face of His throne, and spreads His cloud over it ... Indeed, these are the mere edges of His ways, and how small a whisper we hear of Him! But the thunder of His power who can understand," Job26:8,9,14. But that which we can know about God leaves us without any excuses.

Ways God Reveals Himself

"For since the creation of the world His invisible attributes are clearly seen, being understood by the things that are made, even His eternal power and Godhead, so that they are without excuse," Rom1:18-20.

Adam had a perfect knowledge of God. Adam's sons, though fallen, and even the very heathens have some notion of Him, as that there is a God. And by the light of nature it might be known that there is but one God, who is glorious, full of majesty, and possessed of all perfections, as that He is all powerful, wise, good and righteous: and this is manifest in them, or "to them"; by the light that is given them: it is light by which that which may be known of God is manifest. This is the light of nature, which every man has that comes into the world; and this is internal, it is in him, in his mind and conscience, and is communicated to him by God, and that by infusion or inspiration (Job32:8). For, God has showed it to them; what may be known of Him by that light; and which is assisted and may be improved by a consideration of the works of creation and Providence.

For the invisible things of Him: There are some things

which could not be known of God by the light of nature; as a trinity of persons in the Godhead; the knowledge of God in Christ as Mediator; the God-man and Mediator Our Lord Jesus Christ; His incarnation, sufferings, death, and resurrection; the will of God to save sinners by a crucified Jesus; the several peculiar doctrines of the Gospel, particularly the resurrection of the dead, and the manner of worshipping of God with acceptance. But then, there are some things which may be known of God, without a revelation.

The invisible things of God, from the creation of the world are clearly seen; this is no new discovery. But what men have had, and might, by the light of nature, have enjoyed ever since the world was created; these being understood, in an intellectual way, by the things that are made; the various works of creation; all which proclaim the being, unity, and perfections of God their Creator. Man, reasoning upon the basis of the law of cause and effect, which law requires an adequate cause for every effect, is forced to the conclusion that such a tremendous effect as the universe, demands a Being of eternal power and of divine attributes, and that this is not a mere blind force, or pantheistic "spirit of nature," but the power of a living Godhead.

Thus, the outward creation is not the parent but the interpreter of our faith in God. That faith has its primary sources within our own breast (Rom1:19); but it becomes an intelligible and articulate conviction only through what we observe around us ("by the things which are made", Rom1:20). And thus, the inner and the outer revelation of God are the complement of each other, making up between them one universal and immovable conviction that God is.

God has revealed Himself to every individual, and if individuals, wherever they are, no matter how remote they are, do not "hold the truth in unrighteousness", that is, do not suppress that truth by the love of sin, that truth will protect them from the excesses of sin, and eventually lead them to the truth of God by His gracious Providence. But men don't do that. They avoid the truth of God. All men possess enough of the divine truth and moral law to preserve them from hell, but they've halted the growth and development of those by the love of sin. And the wrath of God waits. But remember, there is good news, and the good news is Christ has taken the full fury of God's wrath if you'll accept His gracious substitution for you.

The knowledge of God is all over, and if it does its

legitimate work, and man allows it to do that legitimate work, it will keep a man from the excesses of sin and lead that man to God. But men suppress it. They love darkness rather than Light because their deeds are evil. "The fool says in his heart, there is no God," Ps14:1. He says that because he doesn't want there to be a God because if there's a God, he's in trouble. They don't want there to be a God to call them to accountability. Man tries to postulate that there is no God, and if he doesn't do that he says, "Well, I'll invent a God who can tolerate my sin." And he clearly avoids the true voice of God.

God, we know You're angry over sin. We know how You hate sin but O how much You must love to have hated sin so much and yet put it all on the One You loved, Your own Son the Lord Our Lord Jesus, for us. O how You must love. Thank You for that love, forgiving love, merciful love, gracious love.

So that they are without excuse: Thus, through the light of the created universe, unsaved man recognizes the fact that there is a supreme Being who created it,

Ways God Reveals Himself

who has eternal power and divine attributes, a Being to whom worship and obedience are due. This is the truth which unsaved man is repressing. Here, lies the just condemnation of the entire race, since it has not lived up to the light which it has. This, St Paul says, renders man without excuse. the very heathens, who have only the light of nature, and are destitute of a revelation, have no pretext for their idolatrous practices, and vicious lives; nor have they, nor will they have anything to object to God's righteous judgment against them, or why they should not be condemned. All their degeneracy is a voluntary departure from truth that is brightly revealed to the unsophisticated spirit.

St Paul connects the observing of the mighty and beautiful things of the universe with the consciousness of a personal God. Human science, through its telescope, observes the vast courses of the stars, moving with amazing accuracy in their orbits, but often counts it a mark of wisdom to doubt whether an intelligent Being exists at all! No really great scientist today supports the Darwinian Theory; and some of the most prominent scientific men are saying, "There must be a God, a Creator." The basic reason for all evolutionary religion, from atheism and humanism to ancient Babylonian paganism to modern New Age pantheism is that men and women did not like to believe in the God of creation. They are forced then to find some evolutionary explanation for the world with which they could be more comfortable to explain so wondrous a Creation.

Men are judged and sent to hell not because they do not live up to the light evidenced in the universe but because ultimately that rejection leads them to reject Our Lord Jesus Christ...if a person lives up to the light of the revelation he has, God will provide for his hearing the Gospel by some means or another. Because the Ethiopian eunuch was sincerely seeking God, the Holy Spirit sent St Philip to witness to him. Upon hearing the Gospel, he believed and was baptized (Acts8:26-39). Because Cornelius, a Gentile centurion in the Roman army, was "a devout man, and one who feared God with all his household, and gave many alms to the Jewish people, and prayed to God continually", God sent St Peter to him to explain the Gospel. "While Peter was still speaking, the Holy Spirit fell upon all those who were listening to the message," and they were "baptized in the name of Our Lord Jesus Christ" (Acts10:2, 44, and 48). Because Lydia was a true worshiper of God, when she heard the Gospel, "the Lord opened her heart to respond to the things spoken by Paul" (Acts16:14).

Years ago, the Trans World Radio dropped transistor radios into the jungle. It wasn't until several years later that missionaries finally reached these isolated tribes only to find that some of these pagans had become believers through the message broadcast on the transistor radio! God wants none to perish but for all to come to repentance (2Pt3:9).

If a man or woman does not suppress God's truth but in fact seeks Him, it is God's responsibility to provide a witness either in His Word or through a missionary sent to that person to proclaim the good news of Our Lord Jesus Christ. This truth addresses and refutes the argument of so many as to "what about those who have never heard."

Therefore, the Bible says that God has revealed Himself through nature.

OUR CONSCIENCE TELLS US THAT GOD EXISTS

God has also revealed Himself through the spirit, or mind, of humanity. All societies have a certain moral code built into them in which stealing, lying, murder, and such are universally condemned. Humanity's sense of right and wrong testifies to God's existence. The Apostle Paul wrote:

"For when Gentiles, who do not have the Law, by nature do the things contained in the Law, these although not having the Law are a law to themselves, who show the work of the Law written in their hearts, their conscience also bearing witness, and between themselves their thoughts accusing or else excusing them," Rom2:14,15. The conscience is a God-given capacity for human beings to exercise self-evaluation. The conscience is defined as that part of the human psyche that induces mental anguish and feelings of guilt when we violate it and feelings of pleasure and well-being when our actions, thoughts and words are in conformity to our value systems.

The conscience is the part of the human soul that is most like God (Gn3:22). The conscience of man was awakened when Adam and Eve disobeyed God's command and ate from the tree of the knowledge of good and evil (Gn3:6). Before that, they had known only good. When we choose to "know" evil by intimate experience, our consciences are violated and emotional discomfort takes over. Because God has created us as moral beings who are personally accountable to Him, and created us for fellowship with Him, He has given us a built-in moral conscience. When we do wrong, we sense that we are at odds with our created purpose, and that feeling is deeply disturbing.

In Romans 2, St Paul is speaking about those peoples of the world who have never had the privilege of being given God's moral law as the Jewish people had. He says, "Some people naturally obey the Law's commands, even though they don't have the Law. This proves that the conscience is like a law written in the human heart. And it will show whether we are forgiven or condemned, when God has Our Lord Jesus Christ judge everyone's secret thoughts. The problem, however, is that we live in a fallen world where we have all been infected by Sin, and one of the results is that our conscience gets distorted too. Our conscience is a bit like an alarm clock. We are very good at rationalising our behaviour and we can reset it and make it go off when we want!

The Bible talks about a "good conscience" (1Ti1:5), and a "clear conscience" (1Ti3:9), but it also talks about a "weak conscience" (1Co8:12), a "seared" conscience (1Ti4:2), a "corrupted" conscience (Tit1:15) and "an evil conscience" (Heb10:22). Our conscience can be desensitised if we fail to listen to it, even to the extent that we become morally blind, stumbling around in moral darkness as St John puts it (1Jn2:11).

A conscience that is "seared" is one that is rendered insensitive as though it had been cauterized with a hot iron (1Ti4:1-2). Such a conscience is hardened and calloused, no longer feeling anything. A person with a seared conscience no longer listens to its promptings, and he can sin with abandon, delude himself into thinking all is well with his soul, and treat others insensitively and without compassion.

The conscience which is corrupt and defiled (Tts1:15), is one that is being naturally unable to do its office; it remains sleepy and inactive. But because there is a false light in the dark mind, the natural conscience following the same darkness will call evil good, and good evil (Is5:20). "Whosoever kills you will think that he does God service," Jn16:2. An "evil conscience" is a consciousness of evil, or a conscience oppressed with sin; that is, a conscience that accuses of guilt. We are made free from such a conscience through the atonement of Our Lord Jesus.

The conscience is a servant of the individual's value system. An immature or weak value system produces a weak conscience, while a fully informed value system produces a strong sense of right and wrong. In the Christian life, one's conscience can be driven by an inadequate understanding of scriptural truths and can produce feelings of guilt and shame disproportionate to the issues at hand. Maturing in the faith strengthens the conscience

Because we do have consciences, however, and because we really are accountable to God, it means that guilt is something very real. Because the whole concept of sin and accountability tends to be rubbished today, all feelings of guilt tend to be written off as psychological problems. We need a psychiatrist, not a minister of the Gospel! Now it is certainly possible to have exaggerated or unreal feelings of guilt. But this does not negate the real thing. Christianity not only takes guilt seriously, but it has an answer for it in confession, repentance and the acceptance of forgiveness through the Cross of Christ. When we fail morally we can dismiss it, we can deny it, we can distort it, or we can deal with it.

A healthy conscience discerns between good and evil, and it gets weighed down with guilt over wrongdoing. This sense of guilt should motivate you to take responsibility for your actions and seek forgiveness when you have done something wrong. You will gain a clear conscience when your sin is pardoned and its accompanying guilt is resolved through genuine repentance.

A clear conscience before God is possible through faith in Our Lord Jesus Christ for salvation. When you receive God's gift of salvation, your sins are forgiven and your relationship with God is restored. A clear conscience before other people comes through the repentance and restitution that restore damaged relationships.

Because our conscience is not sufficient guide in itself to living as God intended we should, if we want to live in a meaningful relationship with Him, we need some clearer guidelines. God has given us these through the inspired writers of the Bible as St Paul puts it in writing to his younger disciple, Timothy. Everything in the Scriptures is God's Word. All of it is useful for teaching and helping people and for correcting them and showing them how to live. The Scriptures train God's servants to do all kinds of good deeds (2Ti3:16, 17). What are these guidelines?

If we deny the reality of sin and guilt and our accountability to God, then we have no way of dealing with it. Our mental homes are full of people who would not be there if they knew they were forgiven.

It was God whom Adam and Eve had offended; yet God Himself provided the solution to their violated consciences. He slaughtered an innocent animal to cover their nakedness (Gn3:21). This was a foreshadowing of God's intended plan to cover the sin of all mankind. Humans have tried a variety of things to clear their consciences, from charity work to self-mutilation. History is replete with examples of mankind's efforts to appease his conscience, but nothing works. So, he often turns to other means of drowning out that inner voice that declares him guilty. Addictions, immorality, violence, and greed are often deeply rooted in the fertile soil of a guilty conscience.

However, since all sin is ultimately a sin against God, only God can redeem a violated conscience. Just as He did in the Garden of Eden, God provides us a covering through the sacrifice of something perfect and blameless (Ex12:5; Lv9:3; 1Pt1:18–19). God sent His Own Son Our Lord Jesus into the world for the purpose of being the final, perfect sacrifice for the sins of the whole world (Jn3:16; 1Jn2:2). When Our Lord Jesus went to the Cross, He took upon Himself every sin we would ever commit. Every violated conscience, every sinful thought, and every evil act was placed upon Him (1Pt2:24). All the righteous wrath that God has for our sin was poured out on His Own

Son (Is53:6; Jn3:36). Just as an innocent animal was sacrificed to cover Adam's sin, so the perfect Son was sacrificed to cover ours. God Himself chooses to make us right with Him and pronounce us forgiven.

We can have our consciences cleansed when we bring our sin, our failures, and our miserable attempts to appease God to the foot of the Cross. The atonement of Christ forgives our sin and cleanses our conscience (Heb10:22). We acknowledge our inability to cleanse our own hearts and ask Him to do it for us. We trust that Our Lord Jesus' death and resurrection are sufficient to pay the price we owe God. When we accept Our Lord Jesus' payment for our personal sin, God promises to cast our sins away from us "as far as the east is from the west" (Ps103:12; Heb8:12).

In Christ, we are freed from the stranglehold of sin. We are set free to pursue righteousness and purity and become the men and women God created us to be (Rom6:18). As followers of Christ, we will still commit occasional sin. But, even then, God provides a way for us to have our consciences cleared. "If we confess our sin, he is faithful and just to forgive our sin and to cleanse us from all unrighteousness," 1Jn1:9. Often with that confession, there comes the knowledge that we must make things right with the ones we have offended. We can take that step with the people we have hurt, knowing that God has already forgiven us.

Our consciences can remain clear as we continually confess our sin to God and trust that the blood of Our Lord Jesus is sufficient to make us right with Him. We continue to "seek first the kingdom of God and His righteousness" (Mt6:33). We trust that, in spite of our imperfections, God delights in us and in His transforming work in our lives (Php2:13; Rom8:29). Our Lord Jesus said, "So if the Son makes you free, you will be free indeed," Jn8:36. We live with a clear conscience by refusing to wallow in the failures that God has forgiven. We stand confident in His promise that, "if God is for us, who can be against us?" (Rom8:31).

When we have a good conscience, we have God's peace. A good conscience is a necessary quality of purity to be maintained before our pure and holy God. It is through our personal commitment, devotion, and obedience to Christ Our Lord Jesus, that we are kept within the Father's peace and in His blessing: "the peace of God, which passes all understanding, shall keep your hearts and minds through Christ Jesus," Php4:7. Having the peace of God, and having a good conscience, are some of the initial (and most-desirable) fruits of being baptized with water and the Spirit.

As Christians, we are to keep, as our first priority, our consciences clear by obeying God and keeping our relationship with Him in good standing. We do this by the application of His Word, renewing and softening our hearts continually. We consider those whose consciences are weak, treating them with Christian love and compassion. It takes effort and humility to maintain a clear conscience, but it is worth the investment. "He that covers his sins shall not prosper: but whosoever confesses and forsakes them shall have mercy," Pr28:13.

JESUS REVEALS GOD TO US

When the Saviour came, He not only spoke God's Word to us but He revealed God's nature (Heb1:2). The Son of God is God's final revelation to us. He is the fullest revelation of God that we will ever have here on earth. Do you not see why Satan has tried through the centuries to distort and deny who Jesus really is?

God has also revealed Himself to the world through the person of Jesus Christ. Jesus Himself testified that He had come to earth to reveal the will of God the Father. "All things have been delivered to Me by My Father, and no one knows the Son except the Father. Nor does anyone know the Father except the Son, and he to whom the Son wills to reveal Him," Mt11:27. Jesus is the one who reveals God to us. If we want to know what God is like, all we have to do is look at Jesus. If we want to know how God cares for people, we can look at how Jesus ministered to them. If we want to know God's will for our lives, we can listen to Jesus' words and know they reveal God's truth. Jesus reveals the nature of God in His actions and His words. And, Jesus continues to reveal God to us. He is the one through whom the fullest revelation of God comes.

The Son of God is the Word (Jn1:1). Words reveal our invisible thoughts. In the same way Jesus made the invisible God visible. How did He do it? "And the Word became flesh and dwelt among us, and we beheld His glory, the glory as of the only begotten of the Father, full of grace and truth.... No one has seen God at any time. The only begotten Son, who is in the bosom of the Father, He has declared Him," Jn1:14, 18.

When did the Word become flesh? When did God become a human being? God the Son became a man when the Holy Spirit overshadowed St Mary and placed in her womb the Holy one who was the Son of God. When Jesus Christ was born 2000 years ago, God entered this physical world and lived among us. No one has ever seen God's essence but God the Son has made Him visible and knowable. He said Himself, "Anyone who has seen Me has seen the Father," Jn14:9.

"But Jesus answered them, 'My Father has been working until now, and I have been working.' Therefore, the Jews sought all the more to kill Him, because He not only broke the Sabbath, but also said that God was His Father, making Himself equal with God. Then Jesus answered and said to them, 'Most assuredly, I say to you, the Son can do nothing of Himself, but what He sees the Father do; for whatever He does, the Son also does in like manner. For the Father loves the Son, and shows Him all things that He Himself does; and He will show Him greater works than these, that you may marvel. For as the Father raises the dead and gives life to them, even so the Son gives life to whom He will. For the Father judges no one, but has committed all judgment to the Son, that all should honour the Son just as they honour the Father. He who does not honour the Son does not honour the Father who sent Him'," Jn5:17-23.

Let's look to Jesus if we really want to know God. We are indebted to Christ for all the revelation we have of God the Father's will and love, ever since Adam sinned. Jesus taught about God and the kingdom of God through parables and through His very own life. When Jesus says "I have declared Your name" (Jn17:26), it means that He has made God known to the people. It means that He revealed God's character and His power, and He continues to do so.

Jesus revealed God as His Father and your Father. This means that God wants to be your eternal Father, and He wants you to accept the position of His child. The Son revealed that we have a heavenly Father. And what do we see when we see Jesus? The glory of a God who is full of

Grace and Truth.

As Jesus walked the earth His mission was to reveal the heart of His Father, the God of love. God sent His Son to reveal His love. It is through knowing God, heart to heart, that we come to experience His love. Your mission is to experience and reveal the love of God; just as Jesus did. Jesus continues to reveal the Father through His body, the Church, which includes you if you are willing. Our God is not a cosmic ogre waiting to destroy us but a merciful, gracious Father who welcomes us into His family.

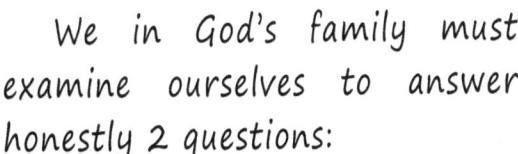

We in God's family must examine ourselves to answer honestly 2 questions:

Do I believe the Bible is the inerrant, authoritative Word of God and totally true?

Do I believe what the Bible teaches about Jesus Christ, that He was the fully human and fully divine Son of God?

THE SCRIPTURES TESTIFY OF GOD'S EXISTENCE

God also has revealed Himself through the written Word, the Scriptures. The Bible is God's revelation of Himself to humankind. The Scripture says of itself: "All Scripture is given by inspiration of God, and is profitable for doctrine, for reproof for correction, for instruction in righteousness," 2Ti3:16. The Bible is humankind's source for the knowledge of God and His plan.

The Holy Bible is a library of seventy books written by more than forty authors over a period of nearly two thousand years by different types of people in different parts of the world. Despite all this diversity in time, civilization, education, background and conditions, yet there is great harmony in all the books of the Bible. There are no conflicts and the spirit of the written Word remains the same and unified. Therefore, the Holy Bible must have been written by God and as such it is the Greatest Book.

The author of the Bible is the Holy Spirit; the pages of the Bible are an authoritative revelation in written form of God's nature and purposes. The Bible is a constant fountain for faith, conduct and inspiration from which we drink daily (2Ti3:16). We do not know how exactly the Holy

Spirit imprinted His message on the minds of those He chose to write His Word, but we know He did lead them to write what He wanted. "For prophecy was never made by an act of human will, but men moved by the Holy Spirit spoke from God," 2Pt1:21.

The Holy Spirit in His work does not by-pass the human processes, but instead, He works through them. He uses living human minds and guides their thoughts according to His divine purposes (inspiration). We cannot have inspired ideas without inspired words. The Holy Spirit was miraculously present, preserving accuracy in the writings. Holy men of God, overshadowed by the Holy Spirit, wrote at His command; thus, they were kept from all error as they recorded things known or unknown to them.

The Christian Scriptures are unique among the world's Sacred Writings. We can have confidence that the Bible truly is the Word of God and that the Bible we read is essentially identical with the original writings themselves. Yet it is not enough to have a high view of the Scriptures. The Bible was given to us for a purpose. God wants us to use the Bible, so that we might come to know Him and to rightly order our lives.

Perhaps the words of Jesus express these themes best. Christ corrected one group of questioners by saying, "you are in error because you do not know the Scriptures or the power of God," Mt22:29. To others He said, "You diligently study the Scriptures because you think that by them you possess eternal life. These are the Scriptures that testify about me," Jn5:39. We do not want to fall into error for lack of knowing the Word of God, yet we do not want to miss its central message – that Jesus Christ is the giver of eternal life.

After we have come to know Jesus, the Scriptures must play an increasingly important role in our lives. Again, we hear Jesus' words: "Everyone who hears these words of Mine and puts them into practice is like a wise man who built his house on the rock", Mt17:24. As the people of God, we must build our lives on the solid foundation of hearing, and putting into practice, the Word of our God.

When we read the Word of God, the Holy Spirit illuminates our minds and opens our hearts (Jer15:16; Is40:8). The reading of the Scriptures itself enables the Holy Spirit to do His work in us, while we read the Word, its message saturates our hearts, whether we are conscious of what is happening or not. The Word with all its mysterious power touches our lives and gives us its power. "You are already clean because of the word which I have spoken to you," Jn15:3. Also in 1Co2:9-10, "Eye has not seen, nor ear heard, neither have entered into the heart of man, the things which God had prepared for them that love Him. But God has revealed them into us by His Spirit". Again, "We have received, not the spirit of the world but the Spirit who is from God, that we might know the things freely given to us by God," 1Co2:12.

When we preach or teach the Scriptures, we open the door for the Holy Spirit to do His Work. He has said that it will not return to Him "empty" (Is55:11). It is the Word of God which changes our lives. God has given us His Word "for teaching, for reproofing, for correction, for training, in righteousness; that the man of God may be adequate, equipped for every good work", 2Ti3:16, 17.

Are these things happening in our lives? Are we learning God's truth? Jesus said, "Your word is truth", Jn17:17. Are we being convicted of sin in our lives and our need of God's correction and God's righteousness, as we read the Word of God? The Bible says, "For the Word of God is living and active and sharper them any two-edged sword, and piercing even to the division of soul and spirit, and of joints and marrow, and is a discerner of the thoughts and intents of the heart. And there is no creature hidden from His sight, but all things are naked and open to the eyes of Him to whom we must give account", Heb4:12-13. Let Job's statement be ours: "I have not departed from the command of His lips; I have treasured the words of His mouth more than my necessary food", Job23:12.

Much would be said about the daily nourishment and reinforcement of faith we all receive from studying the Word of God and the wisdom it provides us for day-to-day living. As we approach the end of the age, persecution is going to be intensified. We are already seeing evidences in many parts of the world. The Scriptures you memorize now and the teachings of the Word of God you learn now will sustain you in that hour, if you are called to suffer physically and mentally for the name of Christ.

If the role of the Holy Spirit is to teach, ours is to be diligent students of the Word. The written Word of God is a living word, "Open my eyes, that I may behold wonderful things from Your Law"

SEVEN SYMBOLS USED TO ILLUSTRATE THE WORD OF GOD

A Sword: The Bible is a pointed sword that convicts the hearer. "For the word of God is living and powerful, and sharper than any two-edged sword, piercing even to the division of soul and spirit and of joints and narrow, and is a discerner of the thoughts and intents of the heart," Heb4:12.

A Hammer: The Bible is powerful and breaks the resistance of the hearer. "Is not My Word like a fire?" says the Lord, "and like a hammer that breaks the rock in pieces?" Jer23:29.

A Seed: The Bible is a living Word regenerating the hearer. "Having been born again, not of corruptible seed but incorruptible, through the Word of God which lives and abides forever," 1Pt1:23.

A Mirror: The Bible is a faithful Word, revealing the individual to himself. "If anyone is a hearer of the Word and not a doer, he is like a man observing his natural face in a mirror; for he observes himself, goes away, and immediately forgets what kind of man he was. But he who looks into the perfect law of liberty and continues in it, and is not a forgetful hearer but a doer of the Word, this one will be blessed in what he does," Jam1:23-25.

A Fire: The Bible is a burning Word, consuming the dross in the hearer. "But His Word was in my heart like a burning fire shut up in my bones," Jer20:9.

A Lamp: The Bible is an illuminating Word guiding the believer day by day. "Your Word is a lamp to my feet and a light to my path," Psa119:105.

Food: The Bible is nourishing food, feeding the soul. "As newborn babes, desire the pure milk of the word that you may grow thereby," 1Pt2:2. "I feed you with milk and not with solid food; for until now you were not able to receive it, and even now you are still not able," 1Co3:2.

The Word of God convicts, breaks, regenerates, reveals, consumes, illuminates and nourishes the individual. Make the Bible your constant guide and companion in life. The Bible is the Word of God; it is worthy of being believed. Breathe a prayer for the Holy Spirit to help you understand the sacred pages. Let us say with Jeremiah "Your Words were found, and I ate them, and Your Word was to me the joy and rejoicing of my heart," Jer15:16.

HISTORY OF SALVATION
IN THE BIBLE

In the Bible, we know about God's plan of Salvation of mankind and how it is fulfilled. In the first few chapters of Genesis, we learn about the creation of the world, life and the first Man. Adam and Eve had communion with God (Gn3:8). They alone, among the living creatures of the world, were equipped for fellowship with their Creator. They freely ate from the "Tree of Life" planted in the Garden of Eden. The fruit of this tree would enable Adam and Eve to "live forever" (Gn3:22).

In the Garden of Eden, there was another tree known as the "Tree of the Knowledge of Good and Evil". Adam and Eve were commanded not to eat from its fruit. The two violated the divine command, and through this act of disobedience, sin (Rom5:12-14) and consequently death (Gn2:9) entered the human race. Adam and Eve fell from their state of innocence. All their children thereafter became corrupt and were separated from God (Gn3:23-24).

Tragically, human beings plunged by Adam and Eve's act into a state in which that knowledge of good and evil was to be gained by experience. God grasps the full reality of good and evil, yet never does evil. Finite humanity can only truly grasp the meaning of what is experienced? In a sense, human history, marred as it is by brutality, wars, injustice, and holocausts, is still plumbing in the depths of the knowledge of good and evil that Eve mistakenly gained through what was desirable.

After their fall, Adam and Eve were expelled from Eden and the "Tree of Life" was guarded by armed Cherubim (Gn3:24). However, they left Eden with a promise of new life and hope of salvation (Gn3:15). The Messiah, according to the flesh is Abraham's son and provides salvation to the entire world (Gn12:1-3).

THE FULLNESS OF TIME

"But when the fullness of the time had come, God sent forth His Son, born of a woman, born under the Law, to redeem those who were under the Law, that we might receive the adoption as sons," Gal 4:4. Since Jesus is born under the Law, He can redeem those under the Law to fulfil His promise to Abraham. God owes no one anything. He certainly does not owe us salvation. Whereas the Son is God by nature, we become sons of God by adoption.

The fullness of time is the right time to fulfil God's promises.

The following table demonstrates the fullness of time for Christ's First and Second Comings. It includes the various steps taken to prepare the right time for either coming.

FIRST COMING OF CHRIST	SECOND COMING OF CHRIST
Establish the nation of Israel, the chosen people of God (Gn12:1-3; Acts7:8).	Establish the New Israel, the Church the Body of Christ (Mk13:5-10).
Establish types of messiah for easier comprehension; e.g. • The sacrifice of Isaac (Gn22). • The Law of purification (Nm19). • The brass serpent (Nm21, Jn3:14-16).	• Natural disasters (Rev8). • WWIII (Rev9:14-19). • Building the third Temple (Rev11:1-2)? • The great apostasy (Rev16:8-11).

History of Salvation in the Bible

Establish the prophetic trail in the Scriptures (300 prophecies):	Prophecies:
• Born of a virgin (Is7:14; Mt1:23). • Born in Bethlehem (Mic5:2; Mt2:1). • From the tribe of Judah (Gn49:10; Mt2:5-6). • Called out of Egypt (Hos11:1; Mt2:15). • Raised in Galilee (Is9:1-2; Mt3:13). • Sold for thirty pieces of silver (Zec11:12; Mt26:15). • His hands and feet pierced (Ps22:16; Lk24:39-40). • Buried in a rich man's tomb (Is53:9; Mt27:57-60). • Come back from the dead (Ps49:15; 16:10; Mt28:5-6).	• The coming of the antichrist, referred to by the little horn in Dan7, and Rev13:1-10, 18). • The coming of the false prophet (Rev13:11-17). • A type of antichrist (Dan8:9-12) is Antiochus IV Epiphanes (175-164 BC). • Coming of Elijah and Enoch (Rev11:3-8). • Abomination of Desolation (168 BC, 70 AD and Nero). • The Jews will believe in Christ (Rom11:25; Rev11:13).

FIRST COMING OF CHRIST

In the Book of Acts7:2-53, St Stephen recalled to us how God was preparing for the return of man to God from Moses to the prophets. After establishing Israel, God made a covenant with him. This covenant was ratified through the blood of sacrifices (Ex24:4-8). He gave them the tabernacle (tent) that He may dwell among them (Ex25:8-9). They were given the Law (the Ten Commandments) which, according to St Paul, was our Tutor to Christ (Gal 3:24). The tabernacle was replaced later by the Temple. God sent them the prophets to urge the people to repentance and assure the coming of the Messiah (Jn6:45; Lk24:25-27, 44).

Man could not go back to God; in His Love and Mercy, God came to man. God the Father sent His Only-Begotten Son to the world. He took the form of man and became Incarnate (Mt1:20-21). Our Lord Jesus Christ, who was sinless, took upon Himself the sins of man and gave His life for him. "For God so loved the world that He gave His Only-Begotten Son that whoever believes in Him does not perish but have eternal life", Jn3:16. Our Lord Jesus Christ builds His Church on the Rock of Faith (Mt16:16). In His Church, we have new time with God. We receive new life in Jesus Christ (Jn1:12-13; 2Co5:17; Jn5:24; Col 1:13; Jn6:47-63; Jn17:21-22). In the new life, we enter a new personal relationship with God that gives us a fullness of spiritual vitality through the Sacraments.

SECOND COMING OF CHRIST

The ultimate fulfilment of Salvation is in Jesus' Second Coming (Heb9:28). Jesus Christ will come again physically in person as promised by the angel who announced at Jesus' ascension, "This same Jesus, who has been taken from you to heaven, will come back in the same way you have seen Him go into heaven," Acts1:11. Christ will come as a Judge (2Ti4:1). He will give us life forever (Jn14:3). We will live again in communion with God forever.

The Old Testament implies a second coming of the Messiah, portraying Him as both a suffering saviour and the one who will establish justice on earth (Is53). Zechariah describes Jesus' reappearance when he spoke of a day when the Messiah will stand on the Mount of Olives, which "will be split in two from east to west," and "the Lord my God will come, and all the holy ones with Him," Zec14:4, 5.

What the Old Testament implies, the New Testament explicitly teaches. A number of events are associated with Jesus' Second Coming: a terrible tribulation; an angelic gathering of the saved; and a divine judgment on ungodliness through war, famine, earthquakes. An empire will be established, and then destroyed, followed by the dissolution of the present universe in roaring flames.

While these events are drawn in clear and decisive language, the New Testament gives no sequence of events. And we cannot be sure how long a time span these events cover. Christ said, "No one knows about that day or hour, not even the angels in heaven, nor the Son, but only the Father," Mt24:36. Since we cannot place Christ's return in any given century or decade, Christians are told to "keep watch". Jesus taught, "You also must be ready, because the Son of man will come at an hour when you do not expect Him," Mt24:42-44.

We look forward to the resurrection of the dead and the life to come. Amen. May we stand firm in our faith and enjoy the forgiveness of our sins through the Blood of Christ by daily repentance. May the Lord give us the strength and grace to tell others about His free Gift of Salvation. May we be all ready to be with Christ when He comes again. "And the Spirit and the bride say, 'Come'". "He who testifies to these things says, 'Surely I am coming quickly'. Amen. Even so, come Lord Jesus!" Rev22:17, 20.

THE KINGDOM OF GOD

After our first parents were expelled from Paradise, the Kingdom of was closed to mankind (Gn3:24). Through new life in Jesus Christ, we are brought back by God's mercy into the new creation, His everlasting Kingdom. The Church at worship enters or ascends to the heavenly Kingdom. We come liturgically "to the city of the living God, the heavenly Jerusalem, to an innumerable company of angels, to the general assembly and church of the firstborn who are registered in heaven, to God the Judge of all," Heb12:22-23.

In this life, we experience a foretaste of the Kingdom in the Church. This inspires us to seek its fullness. The apostle John writes, "Beloved, now we are children of God and it has not been revealed what we shall be, but we know that when He is revealed, we shall be like Him, for we shall see Him as He is. And everyone who has this hope in Him purifies himself, just as He is pure," 1Jn3:2-3. In response to the teaching of Jesus Christ and through faith in His saving work, man can be restored to a true relationship with God and so enter the Kingdom of God.

The following timeline shows the past, present and future history of the ages.

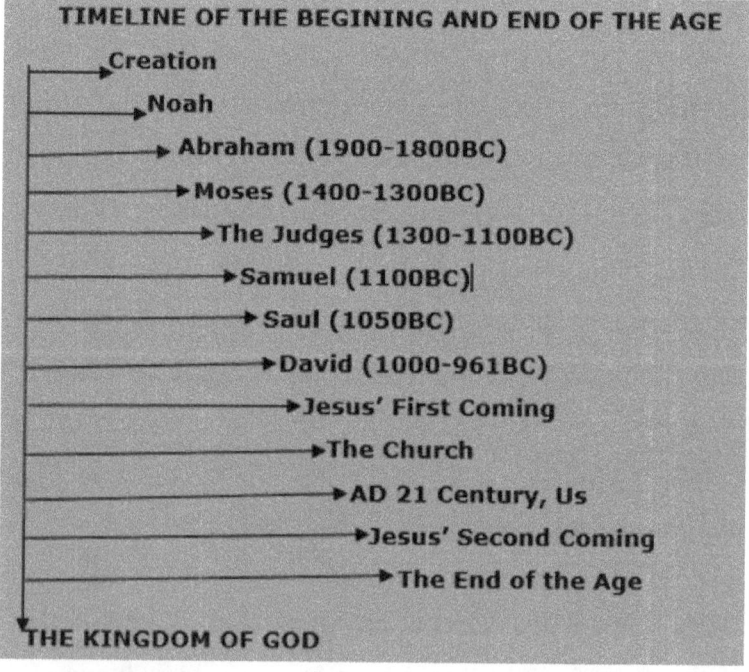

The Bible is supreme, for it has the answer to questions of life and death.

AMPLE OPPORTUNITY FOR BELIEF

God has given humanity ample opportunity to know about Him by means of nature, the human conscience, the Person of Jesus Christ, and finally through the Bible. Each of these methods testifies to His existence. Humanity has no excuse whatsoever for rejecting God. "So then faith comes by hearing, and hearing by the Word of God," Rom10:17. "As it is written, 'how beautiful are the feet of them that preach the Gospel of peace, and bring glad tidings of good things!'," Rom10:15. "The Gospel of peace" is the preaching of the Cross where Jesus bridged the world of alienated sinners and gave the atonement by His flesh. He bought up the whole human family and He bought up all their sin. He reconciled the whole world of sinners to God. Thus, He has brought the peace of God to us who have been at war with God all our lives.

DO WE HEAR GOD'S VOICE?

"Many are called but few are chosen," Mt22:14. This statement is the conclusion to the Parable of the Wedding Feast. Jesus spoke this parable to show what the kingdom of heaven will be like when the end of the age comes.

> In the parable of the Wedding Feast, the king sends his servants out to gather the wedding guests to the wedding feast. But those invited refused to come, some because they were too busy with their own worldly pursuits and some because they were positively hostile toward the king. So, the king commands his servants to go out and invite anyone they find, and many come and fill the wedding hall. But the king sees one man without wedding clothes, and he sends him away. Jesus concludes by saying that many are called/invited to the kingdom, but only those who have been "chosen" and have received Christ will come. Those who try to come without the covering of the blood of Christ for their sins are inadequately clothed and will be sent into the "outer darkness" (Mt22:13) i.e. hell.

Many people hear the call of God which comes through His revelation of Himself through two things — the creation and the conscience within us. But only the "few" will respond because they are the ones who are truly hearing. Jesus said many times, "He who has ears to hear, let him hear" (Mt11:15; Mk4:9; Lk8:8, 14:35). The point is that everyone has ears, but only a few are listening and responding. Not everyone who hears the

Gospel receives it but only the "few" who have ears to hear. The "many" hear, but there is no interest or there is outright antagonism toward God.

"Jesus therefore answered and said to them, "Do not murmur among yourselves. No one can come to Me unless the Father who sent Me draws him; and I will raise him up at the last day. It is written in the prophets, 'And they shall all be taught by God'. Therefore, everyone who has heard and learned from the Father comes to Me. Not that anyone has seen the Father, except He who is from God; He has seen the Father. Most assuredly, I say to you, he who believes in Me has everlasting life," Jn6:43-47.

Many are called or invited into the kingdom, but none are able to come on their own. God must draw the hearts of those who come; otherwise they will not. "For He chose us in Him before the creation of the world to be holy and blameless in His sight. In love He predestined us to be adopted as His sons through Jesus Christ, in accordance with His pleasure and will — to the praise of

His glorious Grace, which He has freely given us in the One He loves," Eph1:4-6. Everything comes from God, and everything should be drawn back to Him. God's intent for the Incarnation was not only our redemption from the Fall but our adoption as sons of God, that is sanctification (deification). The Father chose us in Him, the Son.

Christ who is God by nature became Man by choice. If we chose Him, we who are human by nature, become "gods" by Grace. If we are in Christ, the Son of God, we are sons of God. The will of God is that all are chosen (Rom11:32; 1Ti2:4; 2Pt3:9). But being predestined by God does not nullify human will: in everything God is the originator, the initiator; we merely respond, but our response is necessary.

Christ who is God by nature became Man by choice. If we chose Him, we who are human by nature, become "gods" by Grace. If we are in Christ, the Son of God, we

> God became man that man might become god.
>
> — St Athanasius

are sons of God. The will of God is that all are chosen (Rom11:32; 1Ti2:4; 2Pt3:9). But being predestined by God does not nullify human will: in everything God is the originator, the initiator; we merely respond, but our response is necessary.

"Therefore, if anyone is in Christ, he is a new creation; the old has gone, the new has come," 2Co5:17. God creates life, grants repentance and gives faith. Man is totally unable by himself to do these things which are necessary to enter the Kingdom of Heaven.

Salvation is by God's will and pleasure for His glory. "All that the Father gives Me will come to Me, and whoever comes to Me I will never drive away. For I have come down from heaven not to do My will but to do the will of Him who sent Me. And this is the will of Him who sent Me, that I shall lose none of all that He has given Me, but raise them up at the last day...No one can come to Me unless the Father who sent Me draws him, and I will raise him up at the last day. It is written in the Prophets: 'They will all be taught by God.' Everyone who listens to the Father and learns from Him comes to Me," Jn6:37-39, 44-45.

Becoming a Christian is not so much as inviting Christ into one's life as getting oneself into Christ's life. What is true of Christ becomes true of one who is in Him. That is why St Athanasius can say: "God became man that man might become god."

So, all of God's "chosen" will be saved without exception; they will hear and respond because they have spiritual ears to hear the truth. God's power makes this certain. "And we know that in all things God works for the good of those who love Him, who have been called according to His purpose. For those God foreknew (loved) He also predestined to be conformed to the likeness of His Son, that He might be the firstborn among many brothers. And those He predestined, He also called; those He called, He also justified; those He justified, He also glorified," Rom8:28-30.

One of the greatest benefits of our salvation has to be that of hearing God speak to us personally. There can be no intimate relationship with our heavenly Father without it. But, as easy as it is for us to speak to Him, the average

Christian has a hard time hearing His voice. This is not the way the Lord intended it to be.

Learning to clearly distinguish God's voice is invaluable. Instead of going through life blindly, we can have the wisdom of God to guide and protect us. There isn't a single person receiving the Scriptures who couldn't have their life radically transformed by hearing the voice of the Lord better. The worst marital problem is one word from the Lord away from a total turnaround. If you have sickness or disease, one living word from the Lord will instantly heal you. If you are in financial crisis, the Lord knows exactly how to turn your situation around. It's just a matter of hearing His voice.

Jesus made some radical statements about hearing His voice in Jn10:3-5. He was speaking about Himself as the Shepherd of the sheep and the only way to enter the sheepfold.

The Lord constantly speaks to us and gives us His direction. It's never the Lord who is not speaking, but it's us who are not hearing

"To him (the shepherd) the porter opens; and the sheep hear his voice; and he calls his own sheep by name, and leads them out. And when he brings out his own sheep, he goes before them, and the sheep follow him: for they know his voice. Yet the will by no means follow a stranger, but will flee from him: for they do not know the voice of strangers," Jn10:3-5.

Notice that He said in Jn10:3, His sheep hear His voice. He didn't say His sheep can hear His voice or should hear His voice. He made the emphatic statement that His sheep do hear His voice. Most Christians would question the accuracy of that statement since their experiences don't line up. But it's not what Jesus said that is wrong; all true believers can and do hear the voice of God; they just don't recognize what they are hearing as being God's voice.

Radio and television stations transmit twenty-four hours a day, seven days a week; but we only hear them when we turn the receiver on and tune it in. Failure to hear the signal doesn't mean the station isn't transmitting.

Likewise, God is constantly transmitting His voice to His sheep, but few are turned on and tuned in. Most Christians are busy pleading with God in prayer to transmit when the problem is with their receivers.

"Be still, and know that I am God," Ps46:10. It's in stillness, not busyness, that we tune our spiritual ears to hear the voice of God. The Lord always speaks to us in that "Still, small voice" (1Kg19:12), but often it's drowned out amid all the turmoil of our daily lives.

The first thing we need to do is fix our receivers — believe that God is already speaking and start listening. However, that takes time, effort, and focus. The average Christian's lifestyle is so busy; it isn't conducive to hearing God's voice. All of us seem to be busier than ever, and that's one of the big reasons we don't hear the voice of the Lord better. We're just too busy.

Second, and this is very important, most often we mistake the voice of the Lord for our own thoughts. As mentioned before, the voice of the Lord comes to us in our own thoughts. "God is a Spirit: and they that worship Him must worship Him in spirit and in truth," Jn4:24. This is saying that communication with God is Spirit to spirit, not brain to brain or mouth to ear, the way we communicate in the physical realm. The Lord speaks to our spirits, not in words, but in thoughts and impressions. However, we often miss the leading of the Lord, thinking it's our own thoughts.

I am convinced that our gracious heavenly Father speaks to every one of His children constantly, giving us all the information and guidance we need to be total overcomers. There isn't a problem with His transmitter; it's our receiver that needs help.

DULL HEARING

At the Transfiguration, the Father ordered us to listen to the Son "Hear Him," Mt17:5. The emphasis on "hearing" is worth examining. The Holy Bible identifies two types of listeners. Some are dull of hearing and others are with itching ears.

People dull of hearing have ears which have become so heavy that they do not internalize what they hear.

Our Lord Jesus Christ mentioned it after the Parable of the Soils, saying "And in them the prophecy of Isaiah is fulfilled, which says: Hearing you will hear and shall not understand, and seeing you will see and not perceive. For the hearts of this people have grown dull. Their ears are hard of hearing, and their eyes they have closed, lest they should see with their eyes and hear with their ears, lest they should understand with their hearts and turn, so that I should heal them," Mt13:14,15.

St Paul sensed this problem in Rome (Rom3:11), and also among the Hebrews. So, he wrote to them saying, "Of whom we have much to say and hard to explain, since you have become dull of hearing," Heb5:11. He was telling them that this was hard to explain not because the topic was difficult nor the speaker was ineloquent, but because they had become dull of hearing. The problem was neither in the subject nor the speaker, but in the listener.

The problem of dull hearing starts first and foremost in the heart manifesting itself in the shutting off the ears from listening. There are biblical examples of people "dull of hearing". Cain, after his offering had been rejected by God, got angry. God explained to him his mistake, showing him His readiness to forgive him, "If you do well, will you not be accepted? And if you do not do well, sin lies at the door and its desire is for you," Gn4:7. But Cain was dull of hearing. Had he listened, he would not have perished. God is saying the same thing to us today. Sin is at our door. It has a desire for us, but we should rule over it. "Son of man, you live in the midst of the rebellious house, who have eyes to see but do not see, ears to hear but do not hear; for they are a rebellious house," Ezk12:2.

Pharaoh was another example of a man, dull of hearing. Ten times God sent Moses and Aaron to him in order to free the people to worship God in the desert. The result was a punishment in the form of ten plagues. After each plague, pharaoh would forget and return back to his old pattern. "Therefore I speak to them in parables; because while seeing they do not see, and while hearing they do not hear, nor do they understand," Mt13:13.

Judas the Iscariot listened to all the teachings and all the warnings coming from the Lord; "It is one of the twelve, who dips with Me in the dish. Woe to that man by whom the Son of Man is betrayed! It would have been good for that man if he had never been born," Mk14:20-21. But his love for money had dulled his ears to hear the truth.

Speaking to the Pharisees who rejected Him, Jesus asked, "Why do you not understand what I am saying? It is because you cannot hear My Word," Jn8:43.

Nowadays, there are many people who are living totally for their materialistic desires, love for fame and money. They have developed a dull waxed ear as a consequence of leading such a life. Coming to church and attending services do not help them that much spiritually because of their dull hearing. We need to read the Bible faithfully and know how to relate to the Lord in prayer. We need to pursue passionately the one thing that can truly satisfy the deep longing the Father has planted in the heart of every person. "Have I been so long with you, and yet you have not come to know Me, Philip? He who has seen Me has seen the Father; how can you say, 'Show us the Father'?" Jn14:9.

"For the time will come when they will not endure sound doctrine, but according to their own desires, because they have itching ears, they will heap up for themselves teachers and they will turn their ears away from the truth, and be turned aside to fables," 2Ti4:3,4.

 Being skilled in the Word of righteousness is far more than an intellectual assent; it is putting into practice what God has revealed through the power of the Holy Spirit causing us to be more like Christ. Speaking to the two disciples of Emmaus Jesus said to them, "O foolish men and slow of heart to believe in all that the prophets have spoken!" Lk24:25.

People with itching ears have no tolerance for rebuke or chastisement. Therefore, in order to avoid what they do not like to hear, they change churches, spiritual fathers and seek other worship groups in the hope of finding who would tell them what they would like to hear. Words of praise, false pretences and false fables appeal to them.

Examples of people with itching ears are the youth who leave home in order to avoid hearing their parents, or stop going to Sunday school to avoid hearing their teachers. Also, there are those who leave their original Church seeking another that would grant them divorce, exempt them from fasting or offer shorter services. A biblical example is during Jeremiah's time when God sent him with a very clear message to the Jews to submit to the King of Babylon (Jer27:12), since the city would be delivered to the Babylonians anyway, or be killed with the sword, epidemics or famine. But they did not like this message and put Jeremiah in jail.

SIN WILL MAKE YOU DEAF

Our ears grow deaf to the Word of God because of the presence of sin in our lives. Oh, none of us wants to admit it. We look for some external reason, and we grasp for the newest fad. Yet, the reality is that spiritual truths don't resonate in our hearts because they are tuned to the world. This can happen to the best of us. For example, David's adultery with Bathsheba and murder of Uriah lay hidden in the recesses of his heart when one day the prophet Nathan came in with an appalling story (2Sam12:1-15):

> "Oh King, there was a poor man who had a little lamb that he loved and treated like a daughter. It ate from his table and he embraced it like a child. But, his rich neighbour ripped the lamb from his arms, slit its throat and roasted it for some random guest, in spite of the fact that he had thousands of lambs of his own."
>
> Enraged, David leaps from his chair shouting, "In the name of the Lord, this man shall surly die!" Nathan's eyes narrowed and his finger rose as his voice spoke, "You are that man!"

> David had shouted, "Preach on brother Nathan! This is outrageous! Something must be done!" yet he was totally unaware that he is the lead in the story. How could he miss it? His unaddressed, unconfessed sin kept him from getting the point when the man of God preached.

Sin in our lives keeps us from hearing and understanding God's Word. St James makes this connection when he writes, "Lay aside all filthiness and overflow of wickedness, and receive with meekness the implanted Word, which is able to save your souls," Jam1:21. Before we can receive the saving message we've got to get rid of all filthiness. The word for "filth" in this text is a medical term that means "wax in the ear". The word picture St James uses is this, "Sin in your life plugs up your desire to hear God."

The Scriptures have a bland taste to those who are driven by selfish desires. St Peter put it like this, "Therefore, laying aside all malice, all deceit, hypocrisy, envy, and all evil speaking, as newborn babes, desire the pure milk of the Word, that you may grow thereby, if indeed you have tasted that the Lord is gracious," 1Pt2:1-3.

Craving after God's Word only comes from a heart that is starved of sin and selfishness. The Bible will keep you from sin, or sin will keep you from the Bible. Whenever we diminish the demands of Scripture to fit our lifestyle, sin is making us deaf to the voice of God. Whenever we demote the prominence of Scripture to accommodate our pleasures, sin is making us deaf to the voice of God. Whenever we go days without hearing God's Word, sin is making us deaf to the Word of God.

WHAT MUST WE DO?

None of us is immune to such deafness (Mk8:18; Mt22:23,29), but there is something we can do about it.

Earnest Preparation: In the desert of Sinai God gave His people two days to prepare themselves to hear His voice. They spent every waking hour "consecrating themselves", "washing their clothes", and "separating themselves" so they could hear the voice of God. These physical activities reminded them of the importance of coming before

God with a pure heart (Ex19:10-15). Likewise, we must approach God's Word with a keen awareness that the One who speaks is the Creator of the world and Discerner of our hearts. We must be pure in life and purpose in order to hear His voice.

Honest Confession: We need an honest evaluation of the motive of our hearts, and a willingness to confess any selfish ambition we may discover. The people in Nehemiah's day "confessed their sins" and "read from the book of the Lord their God" (Neh9:2-3). Get honest about the motives behind your actions and desires, or your selfish desires may make you deaf to God's Word.

Have A Passion for Growth: If you have not tangibly and recently grown in your discernment, service and understanding, then you are stuffing cotton in your ears every time God's Word is read (Heb5:11–6:12). The joyful clarity of God's Word is reserved for those who walk most closely to His teachings (Mt11:25).

See His Holiness: When you stand before the Judge your feelings, your pleasures, your wants, and popularity will not matter a bit. We will stand before a Holy God who will ask, "Did you hear and follow My Word?" (Jn12:48;

Mt7:21-23). Then we will know His voice is all that matters! "Who may ascend into the hill of the Lord? Or who may stand in His holy place? He who has clean hands and a pure heart," Ps24:3-4.

GOD HAS A PLAN FOR EACH ONE OF US

As Jesus was assigned a specific task to perform on earth, similarly, each Christian is assigned a special task. It is your responsibility and mine to learn from the Lord His plan for our lives. He promises to reveal it to you if you genuinely want to know what it is. "For I know the plans I have for you, declares the Lord, plans for welfare and not for calamity to give you a future and a hope. Then you will call upon Me and come and pray to Me, and I will listen to you. You will seek Me and find Me when you search for Me with all your heart," Jer29:11-13. Although this promise was specifically given to Israel, it also applies to anyone who desires to know His will.

St Paul indicated that it was possible to know the Father's will (Col 1:9). God's plan for you is very personal. It is just for you. "For we are His workmanship created in Christ Jesus for good works, which God prepared beforehand that we should walk in them," Eph2:10.

God's plan is very definite and specific. "And your ear shall hear a word behind you saying, 'this is the way, walk in it', when you turn to the right hand and when you turn to the left," Is30:21. The Lord guides us by His Spirit through His Word. God's plan is suited to our personalities, talents, needs, potentialities and environment.

We need to become followers of Jesus Christ, ready to carry our cross and be good listeners. To develop sharp ears, we need firstly to pray that the Lord may open our ears like Lydia who "the Lord opened her heart to hear the things said by St Paul," Acts16:14. Secondly, we need to listen with the fear of God, for the fear of God sharpens our ears through the wisdom we receive. "The fear of the Lord is the beginning of wisdom," Pr9:10.

May the Lord grant us to seek and fulfil His plan for our life. May we be ready to carry our cross as we follow

Him until we are changed from glory to glory and become like Him when we see Him face to face.

ALIVE OR DEAD

"Most assuredly, I say to you, he who hears My word and believes in Him who sent Me has everlasting life, and shall not come into judgment, but has passed from death into life. Most assuredly, I say to you, the hour is coming, and now is, when the dead will hear the voice of the Son of God; and those who hear will live. For as the Father has life in Himself, so He has granted the Son to have life in Himself, and has given Him authority to execute judgment also, because He is the Son of Man. Do not marvel at this; for the hour is coming in which all who are in the graves will hear His voice and come forth — those who have done good, to the resurrection of life, and those who have done evil, to the resurrection of condemnation," Jn5:24-29.

"Truly, truly, I say to you, he who hears My word, and believes Him who sent Me, has eternal life, and does not come into judgment, but has passed out of death into life," Jn5:24. Clearly, when it comes to being physically alive or dead, there are two and only two categories of people. Maybe some of you would qualify for being half-dead, but technically, you're alive! What is true physically is also true spiritually: Everyone is either spiritually dead or spiritually alive. There is no in-between category. There are only two groups of people: Those who are spiritually dead and those who have eternal life.

What distinguishes these two groups? The difference is that those who have eternal life have heard Jesus' Word and have believed the One who sent Jesus, whereas those who are spiritually dead have not heard or believed. Jesus' Word stands for His entire message or teaching. Hearing Jesus' Word is the same thing as hearing God's Word, since Jesus only did what He saw the Father doing (Jn5:19) and spoke what He heard from the Father (Jn8:38). And the Father testified of His Son (Jn5:37-38). God sent His Son to be the Lamb of God who takes away the sin of the world (Jn1:29). He sent Him to be the Saviour of the world (Jn4:42).

Hearing Jesus' Word referred to more than just hearing the sound of His voice. Obviously, the Jewish leaders who were challenging Jesus heard the sound of His voice, but they didn't accept or submit to what He was saying. In spite of witnessing the amazing miracles that Jesus did, the Jewish leaders opposed Him and rejected His claim to be sent to earth from God. In Jn10:27, Jesus said, by way of contrast with these unbelieving Jews, that His sheep hear His voice and follow Him. And so, to hear Jesus' Word means to hear with faith and obedience. It means to believe that what Jesus says is true and to submit to His lordship.

Jesus adds (Jn5:24) that those who have eternal life also believe "Him who sent Me." All those who believe the Father, who really believe the Father, accept Christ. It is not possible to believe what the Father says and to turn away from the Son. Jesus says that the one who hears His word and believes in the One who sent Him "has eternal life". God offers salvation equally to all for He created us to share in His goodness and for this end He became Man like us. "For this is good and acceptable in the sight of God our Saviour, who desires all men to be saved and to come to the knowledge of the truth," 1Ti2:3-4. "For as the Father raises the dead and gives life to them, even so the Son gives life to whom He will. For the Father judges no one but has committed all judgement to the Son," Jn5:21-22. The Son fully shares with the Father the divine attributes of both giving life and executing judgement.

SHALL NOT COME INTO JUDGMENT

We are saved because God chose us to be saved. But people ask, "How can I know whether I am one of the elect?" The answer is in Jn5:24: "Most assuredly, I say to you, he who hears My word and believes in Him who sent Me has everlasting life, and shall not come into judgment, but has passed from death into life." Do you believe in Jesus Christ as your Saviour from sin and judgment? Do you believe the biblical witness to Jesus as the eternal Son of God who was sent to this earth to bear your sin on the Cross and who was raised from the dead by the power of God? If so, you are one of God's elect, because none but the elect truly believes in Christ.

The Lord here also gives those who believe in Him great assurance. He says that the one who believes "has eternal life, and does not come into judgment, but has passed out of death into life." Judaism in that day believed that the attainment of eternal life was a future event, not a present reality. But here Jesus says that eternal life is the present possession of the one who believes His word. That person has moved from spiritual death to spiritual life. And if the life that God gives to those who believe is eternal life, then it isn't temporary life. Or to put it another way, if you can lose it, then it isn't eternal.

The moment you believed, God declared you righteous, never to change His mind, as David says, "Blessed is the man to whom the Lord shall not impute sin," Rom4:8. God removes the penalty of sin from a sinner who places his faith in the Lord Jesus as Saviour, and the bestows a positive righteousness, Our Lord Jesus Christ, in Whom that believer stands a righteous person before God's Law for time and eternity.

"Therefore, having been justified by faith, we have peace with God through our Lord Jesus Christ, through whom also we have access by faith into this Grace in which we stand, and rejoice in hope of the glory of God," Rom5:1-2.

Peace with God is now the abiding state into which every believer enters. The sin question is settled. Because the price is paid in full by the work of Our Lord Jesus on the cross, God's justice towards us is eternally satisfied. Peace, as used in Rom5:1, is not a state of mind or heart. Present tense means continuous duration of action. That means that I have it today. I will have it tomorrow. I will have it the next day. I will always have it. It is a prevailing condition between two who were once alienated. Sin had disturbed the relations of Creator and creature. A breach had occurred that man could not mend. But peace has been made by the blood of Christ's Cross. There is no longer a barrier. Peace with God expresses not a state of mind, but a relationship to God. Peace with God is a fact not a feeling.

The Peace of God (subjective) always accompanies faith in the love of God, or assurance of our justification. So, although the apostle's primary idea is that God is at peace with us, it is nevertheless true that inner tranquillity of mind is the fruit of justification by faith. The Peace of God is that peace believers can experience moment by moment, as they walk in the light, their sins confessed and their consciences clean and clear. The peace of God sets a garrison around our hearts and thoughts in Christ Jesus, "when we refuse to be anxious about circumstances", and "in everything (even the most 'trifling' affairs) by prayer and supplication with thanksgiving let our requests be made known unto God" (Php4:6). This inward peace that follows is important, but is not the primary thought here.

To see this distinction and to really grasp it in faith is of prime importance. Until the soul realizes that the peace made by the blood of His Cross is eternal and undisturbed, even though one's experience may be very different owing to personal failure or lack of appropriating faith, there will be no certainty of one's ultimate salvation.

Our Lord made peace through the blood of the Cross (Col 1:20) in the sense that through His sacrifice, He binds together again those who by reason of their standing in the First Adam had been separated from God and who now through faith in Him are bound again to God in their new standing in the Last Adam (1Co15:22). This is justification.

We need peace because of the estrangement between God and man because of sin and so peace in this setting means harmony with God rather than a subjective state in the consciousness of man. Justification has a proper legal dimension, but its purpose is personal reconciliation (Rom5:10-11). Yes, God is a holy Judge whose righteousness and justice must be satisfied (Rom3:24-26). But He is also a loving Father who wants to have close personal fellowship with you.

Do you know real peace? Have you discovered that fame, money, and self-indulgence don't bring inner serenity? Prayerfully, then, you need to make another discovery. Only through a trustful commitment to Christ can you experience peace with God (Rom5:1). Open your heart in faith to the Prince of Peace, inviting Him to come into your life and take control of it. Then, underneath all of life's agitation, you can know the peace of God - the very tranquillity of heaven in the depths of your soul (Php4:6-7).

"Through Whom also we have access by faith into this Grace wherein we stand, and rejoice in hope of the glory of God," Rom5:2. We have a standing in Grace that is God's unmerited favour that God gave to humanity by sending His Son to die on a cross, thus delivering eternal salvation. Grace is manifested in the salvation of sinners and the bestowing of blessings. Through Christ, in Whom they have believed, there has been given to the justified access into a wonderful standing in Divine favour. Being in Christ, the believers have extended to them the very favour in which Christ Himself stands!!! This is a blessing beyond peace with God.

This Grace is given through Our Lord Jesus and gained by faith. Knowing this peace to be based, not on my frame or feelings, but on accomplished redemption, I have conscious access by faith into this Grace wherein I stand. I stand in Grace, not in my own merit. I was saved by Grace. I go on in Grace. I shall be glorified in Grace. Salvation from first to last is altogether of God, and therefore, altogether of Grace.

Grace is the empowering Presence of God enabling you to be who He created you to be, and to do what He has called you to do. God's Grace gives us the desire and the power to do His will. Access to this Grace is access to God. Grace is not something apart from God, but is God giving Himself to us in His graciousness. This is a blessing beyond peace with God. Since our access into this standing of Grace is only by faith, and through Our Lord Jesus, we cannot work ourselves into this standing. Grace is the golden sceptre held out by the King of glory to all who venture to approach in faith.

A standing in Grace reassures us. God's present attitude towards the believer in Christ Our Lord Jesus is one of favour, seeing us in terms of joy, beauty, and pleasure. He doesn't just love us; He likes us because we are in Our Lord Jesus. This new sense of God's presence should be our exceeding joy and great delight. The moment we believe in Our Lord Jesus Christ all of these things are true for us. And they never become any more true - a person who has been a Christian for 50 years is no more justified than the man who just this moment has committed his life to Our Lord Jesus Christ. That is why Baptism is practiced only once in our life. It is one Baptism (the Creed) by which we put on Christ Himself (Gal 3:27). It is a rite of passage given to the Church as an entrance into the Kingdom of God and eternal life. All Christians enjoy these blessings immediately, permanently, and continuously. The question of our going to hell has been forever settled, the certainty of heaven is forever established, and this is cause for rejoicing.

God is well pleased with His Beloved Son (Mt3:17) and God is well pleased with me because I am in His Beloved Son. Our acceptance is in Christ Our Lord Jesus and not in ourselves. God has accepted us in His Son by Grace alone, and upon this fact we must base our faith. There is more in this peace than barely a cessation of enmity, there is friendship and lovingkindness. Abraham, being justified by faith, was called the friend of God (Jam2:23), which was his honour, but not his peculiar honour: Christ has called His disciples friends (Jn15:13-15).

Divine Grace upon humanity, and uses the vehicle of Sacraments, carried out in faith, as a primary and effective means to facilitate the reception of His Grace. Sacraments (carried out in faith) are the incarnational or tangible vehicle through which God's Grace becomes personally and existentially received. The primary initiation into a state of Grace is granted by God through Baptism (in faith), even though, the possible efficacy of even a simple prayer for God's Grace to flow (Baptism by desire) would not be denied. Reformed Protestants, generally, do not share this sacramental view on the transmittal of Grace, but instead favour a less institutionalized mechanism by a simple prayer of faith (sinner's prayer).

Grace means Christ dispenses God's Grace from Himself. Apostolic Churches' doctrine teaches that God has imparted Divine Grace upon humanity, and uses the vehicle of Sacraments, carried out in faith, as a primary and effective means to facilitate the reception of His Grace.

>  If God brought us near to Himself when we were far off, how much more will He keep us now that we are near.... For we were not reconciled merely in order to receive forgiveness of sins; we were meant to receive countless additional benefits as well.
>
> - St Chrysostom

Sacraments (carried out in faith) are the incarnational or tangible vehicle through which God's Grace becomes personally and existentially received. The primary initiation into a state of Grace is granted by God through Baptism (in faith), even though, the possible efficacy of even a simple prayer for God's Grace to flow (Baptism by desire) would not be denied. Reformed Protestants, generally, do not share this sacramental view on the transmittal of Grace, but instead favour a less institutionalized mechanism by a simple prayer of faith (sinner's prayer).

Grace (God's undeserved favour towards us) is not only the way that salvation comes to us; it is also a description of our present standing before God. It is not only the beginning principle of the Christian life; it is also the continuing principle of the Christian life. "We stand" translates a perfect tense, used in this sense of the present, and with the thought of a continuing attitude. This access to God, or introduction to the Divine presence, is to be considered a lasting privilege. We are not brought to God for the purpose of an interview, but to remain with Him; to be His household; and by faith, to behold His face, and walk in the light of His countenance. Incredible!

CONDEMNED WITHOUT CHRIST!

God wants those who believe in Jesus to have the assurance, as St Paul put it that "there is now no condemnation for those who are in Christ Jesus who do not walk according to the flesh, but according to the Spirit," Rom8:1. "Condemnation" here is spiritual death because of Adam's sin. So, those in Christ have no spiritual death. "No condemnation" can be defined in courtroom language. The Bible teaches that every human being will be brought before the judgment throne of God for an ultimate and decisive judgment (2Co5:10), and Christ Himself will be the Judge (Jn5:27). We are all naturally under the condemnation of God: "Whoever does not believe stands condemned already," Jn3:18b.

However, the "no condemnation" involves more than acquittal on Judgment Day. Those who believe in the work of Christ, i.e., that His atoning blood has put the believer's sins away (Rom5:18). They died with Christ, to Sin, and also to that legal responsibility they had in Adam. They enjoyed the words, "Sin shall not have dominion over you, for you are not under Law, but under Grace" (Rom6:14). Finally, they rejoiced in the blessed deliverance from the hopeless struggle of "the flesh" "through Our Lord Jesus Christ" (Rom7:15).

There are those "in Christ" and there are those "outside". St Paul writes that "in Adam all die, so also in Christ all shall be made alive," 1Co15:22. All are condemned in Adam, but those who are in Christ, who also walk according to the Spirit, New Covenant truth, have "no condemnation". There was condemnation as long as we were 'In Adam' our first federal head. But now we are 'In Christ' and therefore are as free from condemnation as He is. We are justified, i.e., declared righteous (Rom3:21-24), now stand in His Grace (Rom5:1-2), are no longer under His wrath (Rom1:18), and are possessors of life everlasting right now (Rom5:17, 18, 21). Christ is the sphere of safety for all who are identified with Him by faith.

St Paul also points out that genuine Christians, although they struggle, will not live "according to the flesh"; that is, they will not persist in a constant state of sinful living (Rom8:5). St Paul encourages us that we need not fear condemnation because we can come to God as our loving, forgiving Father (Rom8:15-16) and can retain the state of sanctity through repentance.

St Paul's use of the word 'now' makes it very clear that living with no condemnation is a present-tense experience of the believer, not something reserved for the future. St Paul was stating that God has no adverse sentence against us once we accept Him. All our punishment has been placed on Our Lord Jesus, and we don't bear it. Those of us who still walk in condemnation are being condemned by the devil or are condemning ourselves. It's not God who condemns us (Rom8:34). God placed the judgment, that the Law prescribed against us, upon His Son. Therefore, those of us who accept Our Lord Jesus as our Saviour will not be condemned, because Our Lord

Jesus was condemned for us (Rom8:3).

To walk after the flesh is to seek to live under the Law. The Jews placed all their confidence in their possession of Torah. They were physical decedents of Abraham, they had the mark of circumcision, they physically performed the ceremonies, and they outwardly did the duties and traditions of the Law. But it was all of the flesh, and it got them nowhere.

"who also made us adequate as servants of a new covenant, not of the letter but of the Spirit; for the letter kills, but the Spirit gives life. But if the ministry of death, in letters engraved on stones, came with glory, so that the sons of Israel could not look intently at the face of Moses because of the glory of his face, fading as it was, how will the ministry of the Spirit fail to be even more with glory? For if the ministry of condemnation has glory, much more does the ministry of righteousness abound in glory," 2Co3:6-9.

 *To place one's confidence in anything outside of Christ is to have confidence in the flesh. To walk in the Spirit is to trust in Christ and His finished work on Calvary.*

Through the death of Christ, believers become dead to the law of Sin and death in Baptism. The law of Sin and death was the Old Covenant Law. In 2Co3:6-9, St Paul said, the Old Covenant was a letter that killed, but the Spirit gives life. The Old Covenant was a ministration of condemnation, but the New Covenant is a ministration of righteousness. Those who have trusted Christ are free from the law of the sin and of the death. They are no longer in the body of Adam, but are in the body of Christ, and are the eschatological bride who is under the Law of her new husband.

 "Most assuredly, I say to you, the hour is coming, and now is, when the dead will hear the voice of the Son of God; and those who hear will live. For as the Father has life in Himself, so He has granted the Son to have life in Himself," Jn5:25-26.

Assurance of salvation is in part a feeling, but it's a feeling based on fact. The fact is Christ's promise that those who believe have eternal life and will not come into judgment. Note that Jesus prefaces His words with, "truly, truly," to underscore what He is saying. Either we trust His word or we don't.

A man once came to the famous evangelist, D. L. Moody, and said that he was worried because he didn't feel saved. Moody asked him, "Was Noah safe in the ark?" "Certainly he was", the man replied. "Well, what made him safe, his feeling or the ark?" Our salvation doesn't rest on our feelings, but on Christ our Saviour. If we're in Him, we're secure and protected from the storm of judgment that is coming on the world. Our feelings rest on the absolutely truthful promises of Jesus.

Jn5:24 is more than a statement of fact. It's also an invitation or call to hear the words of Jesus Christ and believe in Him. Have you put your trust in Him? If not, why not do it now?

ETERNAL LIFE IN THIS AGE

Jesus is the only one powerful enough to impart eternal life to spiritually dead sinners. Jesus again prefaces this statement with "most assuredly" or "truly, truly", to affirm the importance and truth of what He is saying. He used the same phrase, "the hour is coming and now is" with the woman at the well when He spoke about worshiping the Father in spirit and truth (Jn4:23). He meant that it was a present reality, but also that there was more to come. In this case, the "more to come" would be the cross, Jesus' resurrection, His ascension, and the sending of the Holy Spirit on the Day of Pentecost. But "now is" meant that as He spoke, Jesus had the power to speak so that the dead would hear and live.

Jesus demonstrated that power physically at the tomb of Lazarus when He called out, "Lazarus, come forth" (Jn11:43). With the command, Jesus imparted the supernatural power for that dead man to hear and obey. Only God has such power (Dt32:39; 1Sam2:6; 2Kg5:7). But that miracle or sign pointed to the spiritual truth that Jesus has the power to speak to those who are spiritually dead in such a way that they receive eternal life. That is the main focus of Jn5:25-26. While we all would have been amazed if we had been there at Lazarus' tomb, we should realize that the miracle of the new birth is just as great, if not greater, than the raising of a dead man. Just as Lazarus was raised instantly at the command of Christ, so dead sinners are instantly saved when they truly hear the voice of the Son of God. With the command to believe comes the power to believe.

In Jn5:26, Jesus explains why He can impart life to those who hear His voice: "For just as the Father has life in Himself, even so He gave to the Son also to have life in Himself ...." Life is inherent in God. He spoke all life into existence in the original creation. Even so, Jesus says, the Father "gave to the Son also to have life in Himself."

But what does this mean Jesus doesn't say that life comes from the Father through the Son, but rather that just as the Father inherently has life in Himself, so also He granted or ordained that the Son has this same inherent power of life in Himself. It is another claim that Jesus shares full deity with the Father.

At the same time, the verse distinguishes the Father and the Son and shows that the Son is eternally subject to the Father. Through the centuries a heresy called

Sabellianism, Monarchianism, or Modalism has denied the Trinity. It teaches that there is no distinction of persons between the Father, the Son, and the Holy Spirit. God projects Himself at times as the Father, at other times as the Son, or again as the Spirit. These are just three modes revealing the same divine person. The error persists today with the "oneness Pentecostal" movement.

But St Athanasius, the great defender of the faith, used verses such as Jn5:26 as proof that the Father and the Son are two distinct. The Athanasian Creed puts it, "We worship one God in Trinity, and Trinity in Unity; neither confounding the Persons nor dividing the Substance (Essence)."

"And has given Him authority to execute judgment also, because He is the Son of Man. Do not marvel at this; for the hour is coming in which all who are in the graves will hear His voice and come forth —those who have done good, to the resurrection of life, and those who have done evil, to the resurrection of condemnation," Jn5:27-30.

Thus, Jesus is teaching that there are only two groups of people: Those who are spiritually dead and those who have eternal life. Also, He is the only one powerful enough to impart life to those who are dead.

JESUS RAISES AND JUDGES

Jesus will be the one who raises all the dead of all ages and then judges them for all eternity.

Jesus is the Son of Man: The Father has given the Son authority to judge because He is the Son of man (Jn5:27). Along with Jn5:26, this verse explains Jn5:25. The reference to the Son of Man goes back to Dan7:13-14, where the prophet saw one like a Son of Man coming up to the Ancient of Days. He was given everlasting dominion, glory and a kingdom so that all the peoples and nations might serve Him. Jesus is that Son of Man, eternal God in human flesh. He is uniquely qualified to judge humanity because He is both the all-knowing God and at the same time a man who understands by experience what it is like to be human (Heb2:17-18; 4:15).

Jesus will raise all people to face judgment: "Do not marvel at this; for an hour is coming, in which all who are in the tombs will hear His voice, and will come forth ...," Jn5:28-29. Most probably, Jesus' hearers were scoffing at His amazing claims to have life in Himself and to judge all people. So, Jesus warns them not to scoff or marvel at this. Then He adds a further claim of His divine power: In the future, He will give the command and every dead person from every people group from all ages will arise from the dead! Whether their bodies were drowned or burned or eaten by scavengers or blown apart by a bomb, all will be raised to face judgment.

Two Eternal Destinies Only: At the judgment, there are two and only two eternal destinies: eternal life or eternal condemnation "... those who did the good deeds to a resurrection of life, those who committed the evil deeds to a resurrection of judgment" (Jn5:29). Jesus is plainly teaching that this life is not the end of our existence. Either there is life beyond the grave for every person — both the righteous and the wicked — or Jesus is wrong. He says that both those who did good and those who did evil will be raised. The teaching that the wicked will be annihilated contradicts Jesus' teaching. They will be raised for judgment and then "go away into eternal punishment, but the righteous into eternal life" (Mt25:46). If eternal life is forever, then so is eternal punishment.

Judgement Based on Deeds: The basis for judgment will be a person's deeds: "... those who did the good deeds to a resurrection of life, those who committed the evil deeds to a resurrection of judgment," Jn5:29b. This is describing the lives of those who have received new life from Jesus by faith and Baptism as opposed to those who have not trusted in Him. Judgment, as always in Scripture, is on the basis of works.... This does not mean that salvation is on the basis of good works, for this very Gospel makes it plain over and over again that men enter eternal life when they believe on Jesus Christ and are baptised. But the lives they live form the test of the faith they profess. This is the uniform testimony of Scripture. Salvation is by Grace and it is received through faith. Judgment is based on men's works

JESUS' JUDGMENT IS JUST

Jesus' judgment will be just because He does not seek His own will, but the will of the One who sent Him: "I can do nothing on My own initiative. As I hear, I judge; and My judgment is just, because I do not seek My own will, but the will of Him who sent Me," Jn5:30. He not only said that He did not do anything on His own initiative, but that He could not. This goes back to the theme of the entire section, His unity with the Father in all things. Jesus will be impartial and completely fair in His judgment of all people. No one will be able to complain that he or she was judged unfairly. Jesus will be completely just or fair when

He judges everyone. But you never want to ask God to be fair with you! Plead rather for His mercy!

THE BASIS OF GOD'S JUDGEMENT

Rom2:2-16 describes God's righteous judgment, showing how we can prepare ourselves for it. God's judgment will be:

According to truth (Rom2:2-3): Nothing is hidden from God. He sees everything and knows the truth about each of us. One of mankind's great self-deceptions is to say, "Who sees us?" (Is29:15) and think there is no judgment.

According to impenitent hearts (Rom2:4-5): An unrepentant or hard heart despises God's goodness, treasuring up the wrath of God at the judgment. A repentant heart, on the other hand, is grateful for God's patience and abides in Christ, practising a lifetime of repentance, which produces confidence before Him at the Judgment (1Jn2:28).

According to our deeds (Rom2:6-15): The "doing good" referred to in verse 7 is not trying to gain merit with God. Rather, it is the unity of intentions with actions, faith with works. Even unbelievers are rewarded for good works, apart from spiritual understanding (Rom2:14-15). But note the following:

- "Doing good" means seeking God's glory, not one's own glory; God's honour, not one's own honour; the eternal reward of immortality, not reward here and now. "Doing good" is seeking first the Kingdom of God (Mt6:33).

- Good intentions alone, or faith without works, will not save (Rom2:13), Simply to hear and not do is religion without reality. Those with true faith, "the doers" of the truth, practice virtue from pure and repentant hearts (Jam1:21-27).

- "By nature" (Rom2:14) people are inspired by and cooperate with God's Grace. Therefore, good deeds are natural to us, whereas evil deeds are contrary to nature. Because we all fail, we need God's mercy (Rom3:9-19). The presence of God's Law in our conscience (Rom2:15) condemns anything we do which is contrary to true human nature, Therefore, even Gentiles — people not under the Law of Moses; or those who do not know of Christ — have an internal law from God, the natural law written in their hearts, according to which God will judge them. Melchizedek, Job, and the Ninevites are Old Testament examples of non-Jews who were judged to be righteous. Jews, then, have two laws from God — the Law of Moses and conscience — and are accountable to Him for both (Rom2:12).

- Those who are condemned choose to reject God; there is no automatic, fated condemnation: God's just judgment of us is based on our exercise of free will. Although sin impairs our powers, it does not destroy God's image in us or our free will.

By Our Lord Jesus Christ: "In the day when God will judge the secrets of men by Jesus Christ, according to my Gospel," Rom2:16: In the Day of Judgment we are not judged directly by God the Father, whom we cannot see, but by the Incarnate Son whom we do see, Christ Jesus (Acts17:31; Jn3:16-21, 35, 36). Christ will judge on the basis of the light He Himself has given to each of us (Jn1:9) and our response to His light. While Christ came to save and not to condemn, man has free will. Thus, he can reject this gift and he becomes condemned by his own rejection (Jn3:16-21). "The secrets of men" are "the thoughts and intents of the heart" (Heb4:12).

WILL CHRISTIANS BE JUDGED?

Our judgment will be after we die. "It is appointed for men to die once and after this comes judgment," Heb9:27. Before we enter the final state of glory with our resurrection bodies, we will stand before Christ as Judge. Why will Christians be judged if in fact Christ has already been judged for us (Rom5:8-9), and if there is now no condemnation for those who are in Christ Jesus (Rom8:1)? "For we must all appear before the judgment seat of Christ that each one may be recompensed for his deeds in the body, according to what he has done, whether good or bad," 2Co5:10. All Christians will stand before Christ as judge. "We must all appear before the judgment seat of Christ": Not just unbelievers, but "we" and not some of us, but "all of us".

AIM OF JUDGMENT

When we stand before Christ as Judge, we will be judged according to our deeds in this life (2Co5:10). This is not an isolated teaching in the New Testament. Our Lord Jesus said, "The Son of Man is going to come in the glory of His Father with His angels; and will then recompense every person according to his deeds," Mt16:27. And in the very last chapter of the Bible Our Lord Jesus said, "Behold, I am coming quickly, and my reward is with Me, to render to every person according to what he has done," Rev22:12. In other words, the way you live is not unimportant.

Our deeds will reveal who enters the age to come, and our deeds will reveal the measure of our reward in the age to come. This sounds to many Christians like a contradiction of salvation by Grace through faith. Eph2:8-9 says, "By Grace are you saved through faith, and that not of yourselves, it is the gift of God — not of works lest anyone should boast." Salvation is not "of works." That is, works do not earn salvation. Works do not put God in our debt so that He must pay wages. That would contradict Grace. "The wages of sin is death, but the free gift of God is eternal life, through Jesus Christ," Rom6:23. Grace gives salvation as a free gift to be received by faith, not earned by works.

How then can I say that the judgment of believers will not only be the public declaration of the measure of our reward in the kingdom of God according to our deeds, but will also be the public declaration of our salvation — our entering the kingdom — according to our deeds? The answer in a couple sentences is that our deeds will be the public evidence brought forth in Christ's courtroom to demonstrate that our faith is real. And our deeds will be the public evidence brought forth to demonstrate the varying measures of our obedience of faith (Rom12:3; 1Th1:3; 2Th1:11). In other words, salvation is by faith, and rewards are by faith, but the evidence of invisible faith in the judgment hall of Christ will be a transformed life. Our deeds are not the basis of our salvation; they are the evidence of our salvation. They are not foundation, they are demonstration.

There is teaching both in St Paul's writings and in the words of Our Lord Jesus Christ that believers will receive differing rewards in accord with the degree that their faith expresses itself in acts of service and love and righteousness. For example, in 1Co3:8 St Paul says, "He who plants and he who waters are one; but each will receive his own reward according to his own labour." And in Eph6:8 St Paul says, "Whatever good thing each one does, this he will receive back from the Lord."

In the Parable of the Talents (Lk19:12–27) Our Lord Jesus compares His going to heaven and returning to a nobleman who went away and gave to ten of his servants one mina (dollar) each with the command to trade with them so that his estate would be advanced in his absence.

When he returns, one had traded so as to turn his mina (dollar) into ten. And the nobleman says that his reward will be to have authority over ten cities. Another had turned his mina (dollar) into five. And the nobleman said that his reward would be to have authority over five cities. Another had just kept the mina (dollar) and done nothing with it. To this one the nobleman said, "I will condemn you from your own mouth." And he took the one mina (dollar) from him.

SALVATION DEMONSTRATED BY DEEDS

Now what the Parable of the Talents teaches is the same thing St Paul taught, namely, that there are varying degrees of reward for the faithfulness of our lives. But it also moves beyond that and also teaches that there is a loss not only of reward but of eternity for those who claim to be faithful but do nothing to show that they prize God's gifts and love the Giver. That's the point of the third servant who did nothing with his gift. He did not just lose his reward, he lost his life. Our Lord Jesus says in Mt25:30, "Cast out that slave into outer darkness; in that place, there will be weeping and gnashing of teeth."

The first purpose of the Judgment is that the Judgment makes a public demonstration of the varying degrees of reward that Christians receive for the exercise of their faith in obedience. The second purpose of the Judgment is to declare openly the reality of the faith and the salvation of God's people by the evidence of their deeds. Salvation is owned by faith. Salvation is shown by deeds. So, when St Paul says we "will be recompensed . . . according to what we have done" (1Co5:10) he not only means that our rewards will accord with our deeds, but also our salvation will accord with our deeds.

There are numerous texts that point in this direction. St Paul refers to "the revelation of the righteous Judgment of God" and then says, "(God) will render to every man according to his deeds: to those who by perseverance in doing good seek for glory and honour and immortality (He will render) eternal life; but to those who . . . do not obey the truth . . . (He will render) wrath and indignation," Rom2:6-8. In other words, the Judgment is "according to what a person has done". But here the issue is eternal life versus wrath.

Several times St Paul listed certain kinds of deeds and said, "those who do such things shall not inherit the kingdom of God" (Gal 5:21; 1Co6:9-10). In other words, when these deeds are exposed at the Judgment as a person's way of life, they will be the evidence that their faith is dead and they will not be saved. As St James said, "Faith without works is dead," Jam2:26. That is what will be shown at the Judgment.

Our Lord Jesus said, "An hour is coming in which all who are in the tombs shall hear His voice, and shall come forth; those who did the good deeds to a resurrection of life, those who committed the evil deeds to a resurrection of judgment," Jn5:28-29. In other words, the way one lived will be the evidence whether one passes through judgment to life or whether one experiences judgment as condemnation.

He says this even though five verses earlier He said, "Truly, truly I say to you, he who hears My word and believes has eternal life," Jn5:24 To hear and to believe is to have eternal life — it is by Grace through faith. But when that faith is real — not dead — the life will change and Our Lord Jesus can say, with no contradiction: the deeds of this life will be the public criteria of judgment in the resurrection, because our works are the evidence of the reality of our faith. And it is faith in Christ that saves.

God is not looking for deeds that purchase our pardon in His Judgment Hall. He is looking for deeds that prove we are already enjoying our pardon. The purchase of our pardon was the blood of Our Lord Jesus, sufficient once for all to cover all our sins. And the means by which we own it is faith — and faith alone

Even as believing Christians, we must not take the outcome of God's Final Judgment for granted. In every Divine Liturgy, Orthodox Christians pray, "For a good defence before the dread Judgment Seat of Christ, let us pray to the Lord: Lord have mercy."

You've probably heard the expression, "going first class on the Titanic." It describes those who foolishly devote themselves to seeking after pleasure in this life only. This world and all who live for it are headed for judgment. Going first class on a ship that is certain to go down is not wise! Rather, get in the lifeboat while you can! There's plenty of room for everyone, but you've got to get in.

Jesus claims that He can give eternal life to those who are spiritually dead and that He will raise all people for judgment. Either He is crazy to make such claims or He is God and He will do it. Make sure that you have passed out of death and into life because you have put your trust in Jesus Christ and His substitutionary death as your only hope for eternal life!

TWO RESURRECTIONS

Throughout the discourse in Jn5:25-29, Our Lord Jesus interweaves the imminent with the eschatological. This interplay between the hour that is coming and the hour that is now here establishes an exegetical as well as theological foundation for reading the resurrections in Revelation 20 as an apocalyptic rendering of the two resurrections in John 5. Admittedly, the resurrections in John 5 are clearly distinguishable in both their natures and extents.

Following from Jn5:24, we expect hearing the voice to bring spiritual life. But notice, that He said that the hour was both "coming" and "is now". Jn5:28 and 29 present the resurrection of the dead at His Second Coming. It appears that Jesus here declares that all the dead will be raised at once, some to life and some to condemnation. The two resurrections are a "thousand" years apart. The Son takes men who, though their bodies are alive, are yet in a state of death, and raises them into spiritual life. In other words, the new, spiritual life Jesus imparts to believers at their conversion is just as real a resurrection as the new, physical life He will impart to them at the final resurrection.

The most significant statements are by St Paul. "For

this we say unto you by the word of the Lord, that we who are alive and remain unto the coming of the Lord shall not precede [go ahead of] them which are asleep. For the Lord Himself will descend from heaven with a shout, with the voice of the archangel, and with the trumpet of God. And the dead in Christ will rise first: Then we who are alive and remain shall be caught up together with them in the clouds, to meet the Lord in the air. And thus, we shall always be with the Lord," **1Th4:15-17.**

"Blessed and holy is he who has part in the first resurrection. Over such the second death has no power, but they shall be priests of God and of Christ, and shall reign with Him a thousand years," **Rev20:6.**

The Orthodox tradition is not dogmatic on the interpretation of the book of Revelation, but there is a general consensus on the following points:

- The first resurrection is the spiritual resurrection that takes place at Baptism in imitation of and unity with the death and resurrection of Christ (Rom6:3-4).

- **The second resurrection is the fulfilled resurrection of the age to come (Lk20:35; Mt20:30).**

THE FIRST RESURRECTION

The First Resurrection (Rev20:4-5) is the Resurrection with Christ from the death of sin, it began with the Resurrection of Christ from the dead, and it is fulfilled for the believers in Baptism, "buried with Him in Baptism, in which you also were raised with Him through faith in the working of God, who raised Him from the dead" (Col 2:12); "You died with Christ..." (Col 2:20); "You were raised with Christ" (Col 3:1).

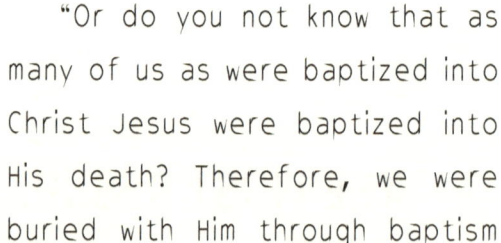

"Or do you not know that as many of us as were baptized into Christ Jesus were baptized into His death? Therefore, we were buried with Him through baptism into death, that just as Christ was raised from the dead by the glory of the Father, even so we also should walk in newness of life. For if we have been united together in the likeness of His death, certainly we also shall be in the likeness of His resurrection, knowing this, that our old man was crucified with Him, that the body of sin might be done away with, that we should no longer be slaves of Sin. For he who has died has been freed from Sin. Now if we died with Christ, we believe that we shall also live with Him," Rom6:3-8.

BAPTISED INTO CHRIST

"Don't you know that all of us who were baptized into Christ Jesus were baptized into His death?" Rom6:3. As can be determined from any Greek lexicon, the original word never had a meaning other than dipping or submerging, and no other term is used for baptizing. The Christian Church knew no form of baptism but immersion until the Middle Ages, when the practice of sprinkling or pouring was introduced by the Roman Catholic Church, which itself had previously always baptized by immersion. The great Catholic theologian Thomas Aquinas (1225-1274 AD) said, "In immersion the setting forth of the burial of Christ is more plainly expressed, in which this manner of baptizing is more commendable." The Catholic Church did not recognize other modes until the Council of Ravenna, held in France in 1311 AD. It was from the Catholic Church that Lutheran and Reformed churches inherited the form of sprinkling or pouring. The Church of England did not begin the practice of sprinkling until 1645 AD. The Orthodox Church has never permitted any mode but immersion.

We are baptized not just into the name of Christ; we are baptized into Him and united with Him. When we are identified with **Adam**, we get the death that Adam brought. When we are identified with **Christ**, we get the righteousness and life that He brought. When He died, we died, and when He was buried we were buried, and when He rose we also rose. We were with Him, because He represented all of us. The Orthodox Church has always baptized by triple immersion, "in the name of the Father and of the Son and of the Holy Spirit" (Mt28:19) and to symbolize Our Lord Jesus' burial in the tomb for three days.

In the fourth century, he instructed his new converts, "You were led by the hand of the holy pool of divine Baptism... and each of you was asked if he believed in the Name of the Father, and of the Son, and of the Holy Spirit. And you made that saving confession, you descended into the water and came up again three times. In the very same moment you died and were born."

— St Cyril of Jerusalem

There can be no participation in Christ's life without a participation in His death, and we cannot enjoy the benefits of His death unless we are partakers of the power of His life. This is the way St Paul is describing our salvation. All humanity was "in Adam" (1Co15:22); now we are "in Christ". And because we are united with Christ, His death counts as ours. St Paul draws this conclusion in verse 4: "We were therefore buried with Him through Baptism into death," Rom6:4. Baptism pictures not only a sharing in Our Lord Jesus' death, but also a sharing in His burial.

In the fourth century, when the Christian faith was preached in its power in Egypt, a young brother sought out the Great St Macarius. "Father," said he, "what is the meaning of being dead and buried with Christ?"

"My son," answered St Macarius, "you remember our dear brother who died, and was buried a short time since? Go now to his grave, and tell him all the unkind things that you ever heard of him, and that we are glad he is dead, and thankful to be rid of him, for he was such a worry to us, and caused so much discomfort in the church. Go, my son, and say that, and hear what he will answer."

The young man was surprised, and doubted whether he really understood: but St Macarius only said, "Do as I bid you, my son, and come and tell me what our departed brother says." The young man did as he was commanded, and returned.

"Well, and what did our brother say?" asked St Macarius.

"Say, father!" he exclaimed; "how could he say anything? He is dead."

"Go now again, my son, and repeat every kind and flattering thing you have ever heard of him; tell him how much we miss him; how great a saint he was; what noble work he did; how the whole church depended upon him; and come again and tell me what he says."

The young man began to see the lesson St Macarius would teach him. He went again to the grave, and addressed many flattering things to the dead man, and then returned to St Macarius.

"He answers nothing, father; he is dead and buried."

"You know now, my son" said the old father, "what it is to be dead with Christ. Praise and blame equally are nothing to him who is really dead and buried with Christ."

"We were therefore buried with Him through Baptism into death in order that, just as Christ was raised from the dead through the glory of the Father, we also should walk in newness of life," Rom6:4. Not only does Baptism unite us with Our Lord Jesus in His death and burial, it also unites us with His resurrection and His life.

 What does being baptized into His Death mean? That it is with a view to our dying as He did. For Baptism is the Cross. Then, what the Cross and burial is to Christ, that Baptism has been to us, even if not in the same respects. For He died Himself and was buried in the Flesh, but we have done both to Sin. Therefore, St Paul does not say, planted together in His Death, but in the likeness of His Death. For both the one and the other is a death, but not of the same subject; since the one is of the Flesh, that of Christ; the other of Sin, which is our own.

— St Chrysostom

    This is our life in Christ, our new birth and entrance into God's Kingdom (Jn3:3), our "newness of life" (Rom6:4). It is our being joined to Christ in His glorified humanity and indwelt by God Himself (Jn14:23). In the same way that we died with Christ, we also rise with Christ into a new life, and this implies that we should live in a different way than we used to.

 Do you believe that Christ died, and that He was raised again? Believe then the same of yourself. For this is like to the other, since both Cross and Burial is yours. For if you have shared in Death and Burial, much more will you in Resurrection and Life. For now, that the greater is done away with, the Sin I mean, it is not right to doubt any longer about the lesser, the doing away of death.

— St Chrysostom

OLD MAN FOREVER DEAD

Walking in resurrection power in our physical lives is dependent on knowing that our "old man" (NIV old self) is crucified. If we don't believe that, then there won't be newness of life (Rom6:4) or victory for us. Our old selves are already crucified. Yet some people have effectively voided the power of that truth (Mk7:13) by teaching that we still have an old self, or sin-nature, that is constantly being resurrected from the dead. There is no Scripture that mentions a daily or even periodical resurrection of our "old man". Only Our Lord Jesus has that power. Satan has no power to accomplish resurrection of any kind. This common belief that people still have an "old man", or sin-nature, does not come from Scripture but through observation. People observe a drive to sin, and they assume that it is their old corrupt nature that drives them to it.

Obviously, St Paul was making a very clear presentation in these verses (Rom6:2-4) that for the Christian, the old self is dead. Christians do not have a nature that is driving them to sin. If that is so, then why do we seem so bound to Sin even after we experience the new birth? The reason is that the old self left behind what this verse calls a "body". Just as a person's spirit and soul leave behind a physical body at death, so the old self left behind habits and strongholds in our thoughts and emotions. The reason we as Christians tend to sin is because of un-renewed minds, not because of a sin-nature.

God made the mental part of us similar to a computer. We can program our minds so that certain actions and attitudes become automatic. For instance, when we were children, it was a major effort to tie our shoelaces or button our shirts, but as adults, we can now perform those tasks without even thinking about what we are doing. It's like it is just a part of us, but in actuality it was an acquired trait.

Likewise, our "old man" ruled our thinking before we were baptised (born again). Our "old man" taught us such things as selfishness, hatred and fear, as well as placed within us the desire for sin. The old self is now gone, but these negative parts of the old self's body remain. Just as a computer will continue to perform according to its programming until reprogrammed, so our minds continue to lead us on the course that our "old man" charted until renewed (Rom12:2). Therefore, Christians do not have a part of them that is still of the devil and is driving them to sin. Instead, Christians have been liberated from the part of them that was dead in sin (i.e., the old self, Eph2:1), and the rest of the Christian life is a renewing of the mind that results in the resurrection life of Our Lord Jesus being manifest in their physical bodies (2Co4:11).

Someone might say, "What's the difference? Whether it's my 'old man' or an 'un-renewed mind', I still struggle with the desire to sin". The difference is enormous! If we still have a corrupt nature, then we are doomed to lives of schizophrenia (i.e., a split mind), but if it is just our un-renewed minds that cause the problem, then we can see the situation improve as we renew our minds. If people retained a corrupt nature even after the new birth, then those who were bound by particular sins before salvation would still be bound by them after salvation. They would just have to refrain from the physical acts, but in their hearts, they would continue to be guilty of committing those sins in thought (Mt5:22). Yet there are millions of examples of people who experience the new birth and are so changed that the very sins that used to enslave them before salvation are now so repulsive to them that they have no desire to commit those acts. They can't even relate to their old selves that did those things, because they are new people (2Co5:17) with renewed minds.

It is truly liberating to learn that we don't have to commit sins; we choose to do so. Therefore, we can change through the renewing of our minds (Rom12:2) because there is no longer a part of us that is a sinner by nature. This is the point that St Paul was making in this verse. To experience the resurrection life of Our Lord Jesus, we have to know that the old self is dead, and then through the renewing of our minds, we destroy the body that the old self left behind, with the end result being that we will not serve Sin any longer. St Paul's point is that just as Sin characterized and dominated every one of our lives in Adam, so now because of our position in union with Christ every believer possesses the potential to live a righteous lifestyle. Before their union with Christ, even man's best was but filthy rags in light of God's holiness and His perfect standard.

Prior to our justification by faith while we were still "in Adam", we obeyed Sin. In other words, the old man in Adam upon hearing a knock at his door, would go to see who was there and finding that it was "Mr Temptation to Sin", would expectantly welcome him into the house. In contrast the "New Man in Christ" can be "rude" and not even answer the door! This is a great picture, for "Mr Temptation to Sin" will be knocking on the door of our heart the remainder of our mortal existence. But hallelujah, we don't have to answer the door anymore because we have a "new Porter" to answer the door for us, the Spirit of Christ in us.

"In Christ", you have a life that is brand new, qualitatively different. How different? In the sense that Sin no longer controls you. In the sense that now you have Someone who lives in you that gives you power to do what you couldn't do before; Someone to convict you of sin; Someone to give you knowledge that you didn't have before. Every believer now has the potential to walk in a life of a brand new kind; new because the believer is now in union with, and identified irrevocably with, Christ.

Will you go back? God Forbid!

Will a prisoner go back to prison? God forbid!

Will a slave go back to his master? God forbid!

Will a rich man return to his poverty? God forbid!

Will a happy man go back to sadness? God forbid!

Will a survivor go back to a concentration camp? God forbid!

Will a Christian go back into Sin? God forbid!

Free at last! I can't go back! I'm walking in newness of His life.

How close are you to Our Lord Jesus? Beloved, if you know Him, His life is your life, His strength is your strength, His mind is your mind, and His power is your power.

NEW LIFE IN CHRIST

"For if we have been united together in the likeness of His death, certainly we also shall be in the likeness of His resurrection," Rom6:5. We shared His burial and resurrection in Baptism.

In the likeness of His death: When we placed our faith in Christ, God placed us into Christ on the Cross, to share His death. By union with Christ, believers undergo a death like His. It can only be like His because His death was the only death that paid full price of redemption. There can be no participation in Christ's life without a participation in His death, and we cannot enjoy the benefits of His death unless we are partakers of the power of His life.

In the likeness of His resurrection: Our union with Christ brings not only justification, the benefit of sharing in His death, but it also brings the benefit of eternal life, of sharing in His resurrection. We are raised to new life for a purpose: union and communion with God. In this sense, Baptism is the beginning of eternal life. For this reason, St Peter writes that Baptism now saves us; it is not the mere removal of dirt from our bodies, but provides us with "a good conscience toward God," 1Pt3:21.

This affects the way we live. We are to live in a way that reflects our future life with Christ. If, therefore, we are baptized into the death of Christ, united and conformed to Him in His death, the certain result will be that we will be conformed to Him in a holy life here (the present life) and in a life of glorious immortality of the soul and body hereafter (the future life). All this is included in the life which flows to us from Christ.

We have "received the reconciliation" that we may now walk, not away from God, as if released from a prison, but with God, as His children in His Son. Because we are justified, we are to be holy, separated from sin, separated to God; not as a mere indication that our faith is real, and that therefore we are legally safe, but because we were justified for this very purpose, that we might be holy. We must be reconciled to God in order to be holy, and we cannot be reconciled without thereby becoming holy.

In the simplest and most practical terms the Apostle sets it before us that our justification is not an end in itself, but a means to an end. Justification was not intended as a license to sin, but as liberation from sin. Salvation is God's provision not only to be declared righteous (justified) but to live righteously (sanctified or growing in holiness). Christian conduct must be consistent with Christian conversion. Do not be deceived. If there is absolutely no change in your moral/ethical life after you ostensibly received Christ as Saviour, then you have cause to be in serious doubt as to whether you ever truly received Christ by Grace through faith. Faith alone saves but the faith that saves is never alone. It can be very deceptive and misleading if the one being described as "saved" has never experienced the truth of 1Jn3:9 or 2Co5:17.

When the apostle says we are to be united with "the likeness of His resurrection", he refers to the walking in "newness of life" just spoken of in Rom6:4, the preceding verse (for this verse explains that). To be joined in life with the Risen Christ, and thus daily, hourly, to walk with Him, is a wonder not conceived of by many of us. But it is the blessed portion of all true Christians. They shared Christ's death, and now are "saved by (or in) His life" as we read in Rom5:10. But not only saved: we walk here on earth by appropriating faith, in the blessedness of His heavenly "newness" of resurrection life! This is what St Paul meant when he said, "To me to live is Christ"; "our inward man is being renewed day by day"; "I was crucified with Christ; Christ lives in me... the life I now live in the flesh I live by the faith of the Son of God," Gal 2:20.

In saying that we have been united (i.e., planted together) with Christ, St Paul compares the death of Christ to a plant to which we have been joined, so that drawing on the sap of His root our root may bring forth branches of righteousness and bear the fruits of life.

— Origen

The resurrection is distinguished from belief in reincarnation, which usually involves a series of rebirths from which the soul may seek release. Resurrection has primary reference to the body. The resurrection is the central, defining doctrine and claim of the Gospel for as St Paul wrote "if Christ has not been raised, then our preaching is vain (empty, fruitless, of no purpose), your faith also is vain," 1Co15:14.

We reap the exact effect of what Christ did. Did Christ bear our sins in His own body on the tree? He did. Then we bear them no more. Was Christ made to be sin on our behalf and did He die unto Sin? Truly so. Then Christ's relation to Sin becomes ours!

THE BODY OF SIN DISABLED

"Knowing this, that our old man was crucified with Him, that the body of Sin might be done away with, that we should no longer be slaves of Sin," Rom6:6. "Knowing this" refers to our understanding that Baptism is a reality, not merely an outward symbol. "Our old man" is our old selves, as we were in and from Adam. It does not refer to human nature as such, but to the power of Sin in fallen man that once held sway over us. "Adam begot a son in his own likeness," Gn5:3. This son of Adam, as all since, was according to Adam, for he was in Adam; possessed of a "natural" mind, feelings, tastes, desires, all apart from God. He was his father repeated. Cain is a picture before us of the meaning of the words, "the old man".

Moreover, since man's activities were carried on in and through the body, he is now morally "after the flesh". Inasmuch as his spirit was now dead to God, Sin controlled him, both spirit and soul, through the body. And thus, we read a little later, in Genesis 6, upon the recounting of the horrible lust and violence that filled the earth, God's statement: "In their going astray, they are flesh," Gn6:3. However, we must not confuse the "old man" with "the flesh". "The body of Sin" is not the human body, but all iniquity.

> Just as he calls the whole sum of wickedness "old man", again the wickedness which is made of different parts of iniquity he calls "the body".
>
> — St Chrysostom

Our body in context refers to our physical body as the vehicle or instrument through which Sin expresses itself and causes our body to "miss the mark" of God's standard (which is perfection, Jam2:10, righteousness, holiness). Remember that in Romans 6, St Paul speaks of Sin as an organized power, acting through the members (arms, legs, mouth, etc.) of the physical body. For example, in Rom6:12 Sin is personified as a "king" that seeks to "reign in your mortal body". In Rom6:14, St Paul changes the metaphor somewhat and personifies Sin as a "slave master" (rather than a king) explaining that "Sin shall not be master over you". Why not? Because its power and claims have been broken by Christ's death on the Cross and we died with Him! In sum, the body of sin is our physical body over which Sin seeks to reign as king or to rule as slave master.

In Baptism, the body of sin is done away with. Our previous slavery to the dictates of Sin is broken. This annulling of the power of Sin is based on a recognized principle — that death settles all claims. Our union with Christ in His death, which was designed to deal with Sin once for all, means that we are free from the hold of Sin. Its mastery is broken (Rom6:7) and our selfish nature has been defeated, disabled and deprived of power. What St Paul is stressing in this great section of Romans is that not only is penalty of sin paid for in full (Jn19:30), but that the power of Sin and its "right" to rule over our lives has been broken.

When we are told, for instance, in Colossians, that we have put off "the old man", we know that we are being addressed as new creation in Christ. Our old self was a descendant of Adam, a body under the power of Sin, and that died on the cross. Our former identification with Adam is dead; we are no longer his, but we belong to Christ. The "old man" is contrasted with the "new man" (Col 3:9-10) which is what we are and have in Christ. The "old man" therefore, is not Adam personally, any more than the "new man" is Christ personally. We recognize the "old man" again in the words "Put away as concerning your former manner of life the old man," Eph4:22. In former times the indolence, appetites, necessities, and dangers of the body ruled us with an influence we could not resist; and led us into sin. We were born with or into a body of sin. But, now that our old self has been nailed to the Cross of Christ, the power of Sin over our body has been rendered inoperative. Sin is now a choice.

BAPTISM: FREEDOM FROM SIN

"Knowing this, that our old self was crucified with Him, that our body of Sin might be done away with, that we should no longer be slaves to Sin; for he who has died is freed from sin," Rom6:6-7. Only a renewed relationship with God can give us the freedom from the cursed, selfish desires that always drive us but never fulfil us. Relationship with God is restored through death, Christ's death on the Cross, and our faith in Christ that makes His crucifixion our crucifixion.

There is a difference between being "freed" and being "free". In the 1860s, President Abraham Lincoln issued the Emancipation Proclamation that "freed" the American slaves. Many slaves, however, continued to serve their masters in slavery because the truth was hidden from them or in some cases, the slaves were afraid that they couldn't make it on their own. Likewise, Christians have been "freed" from Sin, but that doesn't automatically mean all Christians experience that freedom. Through ignorance and deception, Satan continues to maintain mastery over those who have not yet realized their death and resurrection with Christ.

Without the Cross, there is no remedy for the self-ruling and self-seeking motivations that plague humans. The nature of the independent, autonomous self does not change. Teaching people to love and esteem it, might make them feel a little better about the situation, but it cannot change the nature of the problem. This self that we try to feel good about is alienated and afraid because of Sin, not because of a lack of the proper "self-talk".

Many believers are ignorant of this doctrine. Once they trust Christ as their Saviour, they immediately try to Christianise "self". Consequently, many well-meaning Christians spend years trying to make "self" look and act like Christ. Layers and layers of good works are piled on. Hours and hours of prayer are added. All of this is fortified by sermons and seminars and tapes and books, and on and on it goes. In many respects, they are actually hindering the will of God in their lives. Sooner or later, because of His unwavering commitment to finish what He has begun, God begins to peel away the layers of "self". This is usually a painful process because it involves exposing the inadequacy of "self". That means failure at those things that were once considered one's forte.

Oftentimes this process involves a stripping away of self-confidence. Sometimes God moves in on "self" through a person's finances. Other times it is through health. Everybody is different. And everybody's "self" life has its own makeup. But God knows just how to peel away the layers so as to force His children to deal with their Christian life on a completely different level.

"That we should no longer be slaves to Sin. For, he who has died has been freed from Sin," Rom6:6-7. In the death of Christ, pictured in our Baptism, our former selves were given the penalty of sin — death. Since the penalty has been paid, Sin has no authority over us; we are delivered from Sin's bondage. St Paul is introducing new metaphors: slavery and freedom. The one, St Paul says, who died off once for all from the sinful nature, has been set free completely from it, with the present result that he is in a state of permanent freedom from it (as depicted by the perfect tense), permanent in the sense that God has set him free permanently from it.

Sin is not just something we do. It is a power that works against us, a power that enslaves us, and a power we must be freed from. When we die with Christ, we are liberated from this evil slave master. We do not go on serving it, but we live a new way of life. We do not do it perfectly, but this is what the Christian life is for. The body of sin is our physical body over which Sin seeks to reign as king or to rule as slave master. "Just as through one man (Adam), Sin entered into the world and death through Sin and so death spread to all men because all sinned," Rom5:12. Every person born in the flesh becomes a slave to the rule and reign of Sin.

We deserved to die for our sins. And in fact, we did die, though not in our own person, but in the person of Our Lord Jesus Christ our substitute, who died in our place, and with whom we have been united by faith and Baptism. And by union with the same Christ we have risen again. So, the old life of sin is finished, because we died to it, and the new life of justified sinners has begun. Our death and resurrection with Christ render it inconceivable that we should go back. It is in this sense that our sinful self has been deprived of power and we have been set free.

The First Resurrection

The old self is dead, and yet we live; we have a new life, and that means a new approach to life. We must have a growing sensitivity to personal sin and a growing desire to please God. At the time of justification believers are set free once and for all from the ruling power of Sin, but now in sanctification we must daily, moment by moment fight the battle with our dethroned enemy and we can do so infused by and controlled by God's Spirit (Rom8:13).

The body of sin's power has been once and for all made Ineffective, rendered powerless and deprived of its force. "Done away with" literally means "to render inoperative or invalid", to make something ineffective by removing its power of control. Note that "done away with" or "destroyed" does not mean that the power of sin is destroyed or annihilated. St Paul does not teach that a Christian is no longer capable of committing sins but that he no longer is under the compulsion and tyranny of the old dictator Sin, nor will he dutifully and habitually obey this old master Sin as before he was saved by Grace through faith. The present tense signifies this is no longer to be our lifestyle (continually enslaved) and active voice indicates that we can now make the wilful choice to not submit ourselves to the strong, corrupt desires that originate from our fallen nature inherited from Adam. This means that the normal pattern of life for Christians should be progressive growth in sanctification, resulting in ever greater maturity and conformity to God's moral law in thought and action. A slave does what the master (Sin) tells him to do. Believers are no longer slaves of Sin. This former relationship is a "mechanical" impossibility because of the work of Christ on the Cross.

It is impossible to be alive in Christ and also still be alive to Sin. It is not that a believer at any moment before going to be with Christ is totally without sin, but that from the moment he is baptised (born again) he is totally separated from the controlling power of Sin, the sin-life from which Christ died to deliver him. On the other hand, remember that although believers have died to Sin, this truth does not mean that we are in a state of death as far as Sin's temptations and allurements are concerned, as if we were immune to them in the same sense that a corpse is totally beyond the ability to respond to physical stimuli.

Every believer knows from experience this is not the case. The difference is that now when sin tempts or allures us (Jam1:14, 1Pt2:11), we can say "no" (Rom6:12-13) whereas before we died to the power of Sin, we could not reject the reign of Sin in our lives. Remember to first say "yes" to the Spirit of Christ, Who will provide the motivation and the power to say "no" to the strong desires of the flesh (Gal 5:16, Rom8:13). Transgression destroys peace of mind, obscures fellowship with Our Lord Jesus, hinders prayer, brings darkness over the soul; therefore, be not the bondman of Sin. There is yet a higher argument: each time you "serve Sin" you have "crucified the Lord afresh, and put Him to an open shame." Can you bear that thought? Oh!

If you have fallen into any special sin during this day, turn to Our Lord Jesus anew. He has not forgotten His love to you; His Grace is still the same. With weeping and repentance, come to His footstool, and you shall be once more received into His heart; you shall be set upon a rock again, and your goings shall be established.

ALIVE TO GOD

"If we died with Christ, we believe that we will also live with Him," Rom6:8. St Paul now starts to emphasize life. We will live with Him in the resurrection, but the question in Romans 6 is about life right now. So, what is St Paul's point? When bondage to Sin has died, it must be replaced with something else. For those who are baptised, the replacement is Christ's resurrected life. "We shall also live with Him" means both a righteous life on earth after Baptism and eternal life in the Kingdom to come.

Since the ultimate problem that mankind faced was death, the Last Adam had to defeat this daunting and terrifying enemy. The only way He could do so was by dying, so that God could then raise Him from the dead, thus conquering death and giving Him everlasting life. Our Lord Jesus Christ defeated our ultimate enemy, death, and He has guaranteed the same victory to all who believe on Him.

"For we know that since Christ was raised from the dead, He cannot die again; death no longer has mastery over Him. The death He died, He died to sin once for all; but the life He lives (by resurrection) He lives to God," Rom6:9-10.

The First Resurrection

This truth is clearly conveyed by Rom6:9-10. Our Lord Jesus was not brought back to mortal life, as Lazarus was. Rather, Our Lord Jesus was raised to immortal, imperishable life. Christ was never under the control of death or Sin, yet He chose voluntarily to die to Sin for our sake. In Christ, we too can voluntarily die to Sin through Baptism, and as we are united with Christ, we are freed from the powers of Sin, too. As Christ's death is "once for all", so also for us there is never a second baptism. Constant repentance renews our Baptism as we grow in our relationship with God.

In Rom6:9, St Paul was stressing that this resurrection life is dependent on knowing that our death with Our Lord Jesus unto sin is a one-time death that does not have to be repeated. In the same way that Our Lord Jesus died unto Sin once (Rom6:10) and now death has no more dominion over Him, those who recognize their death with Christ unto Sin will not have Sin rule over them anymore either (Rom6:14). "But the life He lives, He lives to God," Rom6:10. So we are to model our lives after Christ.

"In the same way, reckon yourselves dead to Sin but alive to God in Christ Jesus our Lord," Rom6:11. This is the choice set before us. We can serve Sin, or we can serve

God. When Sin offers us something tempting, we are to answer: 'No, that's the old way, and I am supposed to die to that. That is not the kind of life that I want.' If we believe we will live with Christ in the future, we should also believe that He has overcome the power of Sin and death, and He liberates us from these powers in this life. We still sin, but it does not have the final authority in our lives. It cannot force us to sin. We are no longer slaves of Sin.

But the Christian life is not simply a matter of refusing sin, or playing dead. We are supposed to be alive — alive to God, because we are in Christ Jesus. Our desire to live for Him should be very much alive! "Reckon" is an action verb, relating to faith: we lay hold of our union with Christ and thereby lay hold of every virtue. This is not automatic, or St Paul wouldn't have to tell us to do it. We must remind ourselves of who we are: children of the Saviour, not children of the sinner. Just as Christ died to Sin, we are to resist Sin day by day, and this is the new life we are to live.

Many people focus on the death to Sin that is mentioned in this verse and omit, or at least put secondarily, the part about being alive unto God. It is assumed that if people will just die to Sin, then life with Christ comes automatically. That's no more so than physical death automatically producing physical resurrection. God doesn't need dead people; He needs people who have risen from the dead spiritually.

People who are preoccupied with dying to themselves will not experience their new lives with Christ. This verse emphatically states that they are to believe unquestionably, without a doubt, that they are, in reality, already dead to Sin in the same way that Christ is already dead to Sin. Being dead to Sin is not a struggle against or victory over Sin that we are accomplishing; it is deliverance from our "old man" (sin-nature) that enslaved us to Sin. Our "old man" no longer exists and, therefore, no longer can dominate us if we know the truth. It is wrong to teach that dying to Sin is something that we still have to accomplish by acknowledging all our sinfulness and forsaking it. This actually causes us to focus on self (sinful self) more than ever before. We are not to focus on our sins but to focus on our resurrected union with Christ.

Therefore, according to the instruction of this verse, we are to unquestionably count on the fact that our "old man" is gone and just as certainly reckon that our new man is alive with Christ, desiring only those things that please the Father. Doing this will transform us outwardly in our flesh into people who reflect who we already are inwardly in our spirits. A mistaken belief that we can't help but sin is one of the biggest reasons that we do sin. The power of Sin has been broken in our lives, and the only reason we Christians sin is because we haven't renewed our minds with the reality of our new lives with Christ.

"Therefore, do not let Sin reign in your mortal body so that you obey it in its lusts," Rom6:12. Christians should not continue in Sin. The word "therefore" makes our ability to end Sin's reign in our lives that this verse speaks of, dependent on the truth that was just expressed in Rom6:11. We have to know beyond any doubt that our "old man" is dead and gone; then, and only then, will we be able to renew our minds and end the dictatorship of Sin in our lives.

The command to "not let Sin reign" proves that Sin's power over man is not absolute. Rather it is something we allow by our free will. Man's will was the first aspect of the human nature damaged through Sin, and therefore, it is the first thing Christ heals. His healing allows us to make true choices against Sin. While Sin continues to plague humanity, those who are baptised into Christ have the power to overcome it through their union with Him.

"Lusts" refers to all the passions of the flesh and spirit that make demands on the will. In Christ, a person can resist and defeat these lusts through righteous exercise of the will.

SPIRITUAL STRUGGLE IN THE NEW LIFE

There is a battle going on for our bodies. The old slave master, Sin, has been defeated by Christ, but Sin continues to attack us nevertheless. It tries to rule us, but we are not supposed to let it. Sin will take over as much as we allow, so we must resist it and "not let it rule in our mortal bodies". St Paul says: Don't give up. Fight against it. St Peter makes a similar appeal writing that because we are "are a chosen race, a royal priesthood, a holy nation, a people for God's own possession" he urges us "as aliens and strangers to abstain from fleshly lusts, which wage war against the soul" (1Pt2:9, 11). If you really like sin, you are not going to enjoy eternal life with Our Lord Jesus. You will experience it as eternal frustration instead. Sin now has no power to control a believer unless the believer chooses to obey its lusts.

Sin is no longer master, no longer lord, and it can be resisted. Sin (personified as a "king") has been dethroned.

The apostle's admonition to believers, therefore, is for them to not let Sin reign, because it now has no right to reign. The moment we were baptised, we were transferred from Satan and Sin's kingdom of darkness into the marvellous light of the Kingdom of God and now we are citizens of His kingdom of righteousness. Now we are free.

"Do not present your members as instruments of unrighteousness to Sin, but present yourselves as instruments of righteousness to God," Rom6:13. Unrighteousness is a condition of not being right, whether with God, according to the standard of His holiness and righteousness or with man, according to the standard of what man knows to be right by his conscience.

There's a battle going on for control of your body. Will you let Sin have its way, or will you let God have His way? You have been brought from death to life, so let God win, St Paul says. How do we do that? By giving Him our bodies as tools or weapons He can use for righteousness. We shouldn't let Sin use our body parts as tools to make us even more wicked. Instead, we need to let God use our bodies as weapons of righteousness, as people who work for His kingdom. St Paul is commanding us to stop putting the members of our body at the disposal of, at the service of, the sinful desires of the flesh and the devil.

And so the instruments we are to put at the service of God are weapons (Rom6:13) or implements of war, either offensive or defensive. To obey the desires of our body, is to place our hands, lips, etc. at the disposal of Sin to be weapons which this enemy uses to carry out unrighteous war. St Paul says stop doing this! And Rom6:1-10 gives the truths which indicate that now in Christ Jesus Our Lord, every believer possesses the power to stop presenting ourselves to Sin. If we don't stop doing so, it is because we don't want to stop, not because we cannot make the choice to stop. Notice the important corollary thought that if a person claims to be baptised i.e. born again and a new creation and yet truly cannot cease from sin (as their continual practice) then they would be very wise to assess whether they are truly Christian (2Co13:5, as well as Our Lord Jesus' sobering warning in Mt7:21, Mt7:22, 23).

If believers truly reckon themselves dead to Sin, then they will prove their faith by yielding ("presenting") themselves to God. This is step three in the process of getting victory over the old nature, the flesh. Notice that stern "Do not let!" in Rom6:12. This yielding is an act of our own wills, a step of obedience to the Lord. It is not enough to know this wonderful doctrine, or even reckon on it; we must take this final step of yielding the members of our bodies to Christ.

"Knowing that Christ, having been raised from the dead, dies no more. Death no longer has dominion over Him... Likewise, you also, reckon yourselves to be dead indeed to sin, but alive to God in Christ Jesus our Lord. Therefore, do not let sin reign in your mortal body, that you should obey it in its lusts. And do not present your members as instruments of unrighteousness to Sin, but present yourselves to God as being alive from the dead, and your members as instruments of righteousness to God. For Sin shall not have dominion over you, for you are not under Law but under Grace," Rom6:9, 11-14

A key word or action is "yield" or "present", an attitude and action which has to do with one's will. Because of the unfathomable riches of the truths we know are now true of our position in Christ (Rom6:1-10), we need to make the choice to accept this truth into our heart (Rom6:11).

Empowered now by the indwelling Holy Spirit, we can stop yielding our physical bodies (eyes, ears, hands, etc.) to the rule and reign of Sin.

When the practice of yielding to the God's Spirit (being filled with, controlled by His Spirit) becomes more and more our daily experience, we begin to enter into what some have referred to as the "victorious life". Whatever you choose to call this experiential aspect of our sanctification process, be encouraged that this is God's will for every one of His children and not just for a special group.

In other words, looking upon yourselves now as you really are in Christ - your old life of sin having come to an end: "dead to Sin" and now with the potential to live a new quality of life: "newness of life", make a determined choice to place yourselves at the disposal of God. Our Lord Jesus' charge for us is to love God with all our heart, soul, mind, and strength (Mk12:30).

It is true that many of us live our lives as believers with Sin still dominating us, at least from time to time. Day after day we struggle with the same temptations and make the same bad choices. Too often we place ourselves under the Law, and seek to attain victory over that sin in our "power"! We must know that our old self was crucified with Christ (Rom6:6). We must reckon (consider) ourselves to be dead to Sin (Rom6:11). And we must yield (present) the members of our body as instruments of righteousness to God (Rom6:13). In our daily life we come up against situations that we cannot overcome in our own strength, or with our own wisdom. We need a strength and a wisdom that comes from Above, that comes from Beyond, that comes from Another outside of us and yet rises up from within us.

"Do you not know that to whom you present yourselves slaves to obey, you are that one's slaves whom you obey, whether of Sin leading to death, or of obedience leading to righteousness?" Rom6:16. When you have accepted Christ as your Saviour, you have come to recognize your inability to save yourself, and so you surrendered to Christ and trusted Our Lord Jesus to do in you and through you what you could not do on your own. That surrender was, in essence, "taking up the Cross" with respect to your salvation. I have died to saving myself. I cannot save myself; and since I cannot, I will not. I will only trust in the Life of the Lord to do what I have (at last!) learned that I cannot do. This is what is means to "embrace the Cross" in the area of salvation.

And we see that when the death to Self is thorough and complete, that is, when we stop trying to save ourselves and cast ourselves upon the Grace of God, then God raises us from the dead. That which was impossible before is now accomplished by God. We are thankful recipients of His Grace, and He receives all the praise and the glory since we have done nothing and He has done everything. This is the principle of the Cross. It does not matter what your situation is; the Cross is sufficient. If the Cross is the power of God for salvation, then the Cross is also the power of God for your relationships, your spiritual growth and development, your life's purpose, your encouragement and strength, and your victory over everything which hinders and distracts and comes against you.

At one time in your life you learned you could not save yourself – that was the work of the Cross. Now, accept the work of the Cross and learn that just as you could not save yourself, neither can you love God, love your neighbour, forgive those who have sinned against you, cast out devils, be a bold witness for Christ, or fulfil your destiny in your own strength. Just as you once relied upon Christ to save you, so now you must rely upon Christ to live through you every day. Just as you continually rely upon Christ for salvation, so you must continually rely upon Christ for everything else. "As you have received Christ Jesus the Lord..." That is the Gate. "So walk in Him." That is the Path. If you can admit defeat, if you can surrender yourself over to God in the area of "salvation" then you can (and should) do the same thing in every other area of your life

Walk in Him as you received Him: by unconditionally surrendering to His Will, His Purpose, His Power, His Lordship. Embrace the Cross! The sooner the better!

Know, Reckon, and Yield: These three words are foundational truths that when comprehended and apprehended will lead you into the victorious life Christ has redeemed you to live to His glory. As you come to know as best you can the truth in (Rom6:1-10) and then make the conscious effort to continually reckon this true (you accept it as truth) (Rom6:11) and then act on it (negatively = not yielding to the old sin nature and positively = yielding to God's Spirit as in Rom6:12, 13), God's Spirit will make this truth more and more real in your life, "increasing in the knowledge of God" (Col 1:10).

"For sin shall not have dominion over you, for you are not under Law but under Grace," Rom6:14. In contrast under the New Covenant of Grace, God's Spirit within us continually enables us to press on toward holiness. Remember that this pressing on is not an arrival in this life but is a process (progressive sanctification). The important truth to retain is that God's all sufficient Grace enables each of His children to do what He calls us to do that we might be pleasing to Him. If we were under the authority of the Law, then we would be condemned as sinners, and Sin would have the final say in our lives. We would die. But we are not under the Law, and not under its penalty. Death has been conquered, the power of Sin has been broken, and the captives of Sin have been set free!

Since we are under Grace, Sin is not our master. Going back to sin makes no more sense than running back to our old slave master, or for a prisoner who has been pardoned running back to his old jail cell. In Grace and in salvation, sin is what we are getting away from. If it weren't for Grace, we would be condemned whether we tried to do right or not. If there were no Grace, we might as well continue in sin, because our efforts wouldn't make any difference. So, Grace gives us the freedom to escape from sin and to live for righteousness. It makes no sense to seek salvation at the same time as seeking sin.

As Christians, all of us continue to sin to some degree, not because we have to, but because we are still in the process of renewing our minds (Rom6:12). However, when we aren't condemned and feeling separated from God because of our sins, we are free to run to God for help instead of away from God in fear. Therefore, understanding God's Grace and our freedom from the Law is the key to breaking the dominance of Sin in our lives.

We must always remember that we rose from the death of sin with Our Lord Jesus Christ. Hence, we must know that this resurrection was not a confined event that happened in the past during our baptism, but rather it is a continual one that we live every day. This essentially means that, in Baptism, we took a power through which we may die to sin and a power of new life and resurrection so that we may live with this power every day and every hour. Therefore, St Paul continues his talk through the Holy Spirit saying: "Reckon yourselves to be dead indeed to sin, but alive to God in Christ Jesus our Lord... Therefore, do not let sin reign (once more) in your mortal body (which died in Baptism), that you should obey it in its lusts. And do not present your members as instruments of unrighteousness to sin, but present yourselves to God as being alive from the dead, and your members as instruments of righteousness to God," Rom6:11-13.

NEW LIFE: ANOINTED TO BE PRIESTS

The "first resurrection" also includes what takes place after Baptism, when we are anointed with the Holy Spirit in the Sacrament of Chrismation (Myron), so we become anointed and consecrated to God, and our lives to be owned by Him. We are also "anointed to the Lord" with Grace as priests in the Kingdom of God; for the spiritual Kingdom is also the spiritual priesthood. This is the "Common Priesthood" that is shared by all Christians, men, women, children, and elderly where we all become Priests of God through the Myron (Rev20:6). Moreover, as members of the body of Christ, we have a priestly ministry to the world, fulfilling the very priesthood and intercession of the Lord Himself, so that to the whole universe we "may proclaim the praises of Him who called us out of darkness into His marvellous light" (1Pt2:9).

This is, of course, different from the "Ministerial Priesthood" which is obtained through the "Sacrament of Priesthood" and is administered by the laying of hands (Acts8:14-21, Acts13:3, 1Ti4:14, 1Ti5:22, 2Ti1:6) and the Holy Spirit breathing (Jn20:22) on the persons called to become stewards of the mysteries of God (1Co4:10). This priestly ministry is to offer the world back to God in a sacrifice of praise and thanksgiving – eucharistically - as in the Orthodox Church's Divine Liturgy. The universe itself thus becomes hallowed, transfigured and sacramental.

"And I saw thrones, and they sat on them, and judgment was committed to them. Then I saw the souls of those who had been beheaded for their witness to Jesus and for the word of God, who had not worshiped the beast or his image, and had not received his mark on their foreheads or on their hands. And they lived and reigned with Christ for a thousand years. But the rest

The First Resurrection

of the dead did not live again until the thousand years were finished. This is the first resurrection. Blessed and holy is he who has part in the first resurrection. Over such the second death has no power, but they shall be priests of God and of Christ, and shall reign with Him a thousand years," Rev20:4-6.

NEW LIFE: NOT OVERCOME BY THE SECOND DEATH

The chief thing to notice about the reference to 'the first resurrection' in Revelation 20, is that it is contrasted, not with a 'second resurrection', but with 'the second death'. The point being made is that these saints (Rev20:4), though they died bodily, nevertheless lived (i.e. continued to live, as Jesus had promised in Jn11:26) and reigned with Christ for a very long period of time, referred to in this passage as 'a thousand years'. The scripture then states: "Blessed and holy is he that has part in the first resurrection: on such the second death has no power," Rev20:6.

What Is the Second Death? In the Holy Scripture, someone's sinful condition is also compared to a kind of death. It is with this meaning that the Saviour says to one of His disciples who had asked leave to first go and bury his father, "Follow me, and let the dead bury their dead" (Mt8:22). Likewise, He speaks with this in mind when saying, "He that believes in Me, though he were dead, yet shall he live; and whosoever lives and believes in Me shall never die," Jn11:25. The Apostle also had this meaning in mind when he wrote, "reckon yourselves to be dead indeed to sin, but alive to God in Christ Jesus our Lord," Rom6:11; 8:10. Moreover, with this meaning as well it is written to the angel of the Church in Sardis: "I know your works, and that you have a name that you live, but you are dead," Rev3:1.

We read that the "second death" is the destruction of death itself and of all that falls within its territory (e.g. death, the grave, those not found written in the book of life as in Rev20:14-15). The "second death" is the eternal death and torment in the lake of fire prepared for the devil and his angels, as illustrated in (Mt25:41, Rev20:14).

The reason the "second death" has no power on those who have a part in the "first resurrection" is that they have already "passed from death to life" and that the life they now experience is eternal (Jn5:24). In addition, Jesus connects this idea, of believers being raised spiritually from death to life, with the bodily resurrection of all who are in the grave, at the close of the age (Jn5:26-28). In the same way, St Paul refers to believers as having been already "raised with Christ" and sharing in both Jesus' resurrection and His ascension (Col 3:1; Eph2:6).

The "first resurrection" with Christ doesn't come until after the "first death in Baptism", and continues in our lives every day by dying to sin and to the evil of the world. This is also what St Paul clarified through the Holy Spirit when he said: "always carrying about in the body the dying of the Lord Jesus, that the life of Jesus also may be manifested in our body," 2Co4:10.

THE ONE THOUSAND-YEAR REIGN

The One Thousand-Year Reign

The millennial rule of Christ on earth is a heresy which started in the third century on the basis of a wrong interpretation of Rev20:1-7. Followers of this heresy believe that Christ at His return will re-establish the kingdom of David on earth, and will reign in Jerusalem for a "literal" thousand years with the elect.

The Orthodox Church believes that the thousand-year period can be any length of time, and that we are already in the thousand-year reign of Christ, starting with the soul of the right thief (even though it has been already more than 1000 years).

It should be noted that binding of Satan in Rev20:1-7 means that Satan has lost his grip on the souls and his power has been curtailed since Christ completed our salvation. Christ's salvation enabled the free will in us to resist Satan. Rev20:4-5 emphasize that those who reigned with Christ were the souls of the elect who had died not the rest of the dead who did not share in this reign with Christ.

This thousand-year reign of the souls of the elect with Christ is called the "first resurrection" (resurrection of the soul). The "second resurrection" is when those souls are united with their new heavenly bodies on the day of the Second Coming of our Lord (resurrection of the flesh). Obviously, those souls who attained Paradise (Rev20:4) will not taste the "second death", which is the lake of fire, a place reserved for the souls that are now in Hades when they are united with their bodies (the second death).

The divine Fathers of the Church indicated in their writings that the one thousand-year reign referred to in the book of Revelation signifies an infinite number of years, i.e. a kingdom that shall have no end. This we know well since from Holy Scripture it is clear that the Kingdom of Christ is not of this world (Jn18:36). In Holy Scripture it is clearly indicated that the Kingdom of Heaven is also the Kingdom of God or Kingdom of Christ, in so much as both St John the Forerunner and Christ Himself called it so. This Kingdom of Christ will be spiritual and will reign over the internal world of man, while externally being revealed in the righteousness, peace and joy of the Holy Spirit (Rom14:17). Christ Himself established this Kingdom and explained in His parables how it will appear, whom it will include and what power it will possess. His reign will not endure for a thousand years, but eternally (Lk1:33). Its inhabitants will include all faithful Christians from all the peoples of the world (Ps116:1-2). The Kingdom will be over all creation, and it will be a Kingdom of righteousness (Dan7:13-14). It will be a Kingdom made up of souls (Mt28:18) - souls that have already entered and lived within it in this present life.

This Kingdom of Christ, derived not from this world, constitutes the Church, or the Body of Christ, of which the head is Christ Himself (Eph1:22). The adoption and entrance into this Kingdom takes place only through the laver of regeneration (Tts3:5) or birth from above (Jn3:3). No one can enter into this reign of God except through Baptism (Rom6:3), which is to say by being born again from above or being born of water and the Spirit, according to the word of the Saviour: "Verily, verily, I say unto you, except a man be born of water and of the Spirit, he cannot enter into the Kingdom of God," Jn3:5.

This heavenly birth by the power of the Holy Spirit is a true resurrection from the dead (Col 2:12-13), and hence the reason why Baptism is so often referred to as resurrection (Rom6:3-5). Thus, also, it is that the Orthodox Christian Baptism is a regeneration of life and a resurrection from the dead. When the apostle Paul writes: "Therefore He says: 'Awake, you who sleep, arise from the dead, and Christ will give you light'," Eph5:14, he has in mind precisely this internal regeneration and resurrection through Christian Baptism, for no one can enter the Kingdom of Christ unless he has first been brought out from among the dead by Christian Baptism. The millennium is best explained as a spiritual era which represents for the individual believer his/her spiritual reign with Christ (Col 1:13). The first resurrection is for believers; the second resurrection will be for judgement.

The Holy Scripture speaks to us about the thousand-year reign in prophetic and symbolic terms, corresponding to that which we spoke of above. From Rev20:1-14 we can ascertain the following:

- The thousand-year reign of Christ is a period in which Christ has bound the power of the Devil over men. "And I saw an angel come down from heaven, having the key of the bottomless pit and a great chain in his hand. And he laid hold on the dragon, that old serpent, which is the Devil, and Satan, and bound him a thousand years," Rev20:1-2.

- At the end of this period the Devil will again be lord over men and oppress them, but only for a season: "And cast him into the bottomless pit, and shut him up, and set a seal upon him, that he should deceive the nations no more, till the thousand years should be fulfilled: and after that he must be loosed a little season," Rev20:3.

- The members of this kingdom will be those alone who do not submit to the beast and accept his engraved seal, and who have a part in the first resurrection. "And I saw thrones, and they sat on them, and judgment was committed to them. Then I saw the souls of those who had been beheaded for their witness to Jesus and for the Word of God, who had not worshiped the beast or his image, and had not received his mark on their foreheads or on their hands. And they lived and reigned with Christ for a thousand years. But the rest of the dead did not live again until the thousand years were finished. This is the first resurrection," Rev20:4-5.

- Those who were not worthy of this resurrection will be raised at the end of the thousand years, that is at the second resurrection, as this resurrection, relative to the first, is the second. "But the rest of the dead did not live again until the thousand years were finished. This is the first resurrection," Rev20:5.

- Death will have no power over the sharers in the

thousand-year reign. "Blessed and holy is he who has part in the first resurrection. Over such the second death has no power, but they shall be priests of God and of Christ, and shall reign with Him a thousand years," Rev20:6.

- At the end of these thousand years and after a gruesomely violent persecution against the saints, the Devil and his followers will be cast into the lake of fire - the second death (Rev20:4-15).

"And I saw thrones, and they sat on them, and judgment was committed to them. Then I saw the souls of those who had been beheaded for their witness to Jesus and for the word of God, who had not worshiped the beast or his image, and had not received his mark on their foreheads or on their hands. And they lived and reigned with Christ for a thousand years. But the rest of the dead did not live again until the thousand years were finished. This is the first resurrection. Blessed and holy is he who has part in the first resurrection. Over such the second death has no power, but they shall be priests of God and of

The One Thousand-Year Reign

Christ, and shall reign with Him a thousand years.

Now when the thousand years have expired, Satan will be released from his prison and will go out to deceive the nations which are in the four corners of the earth, Gog and Magog, to gather them together to battle, whose number is as the sand of the sea. They went up on the breadth of the earth and surrounded the camp of the saints and the beloved city. And fire came down from God out of heaven and devoured them. The devil, who deceived them, was cast into the lake of fire and brimstone where the beast and the false prophet are. And they will be tormented day and night forever and ever.

Then I saw a great white throne and Him who sat on it, from whose face the earth and the heaven fled away. And there was found no place for them. And I saw the dead, small and great, standing before God, and books were opened. And another book was opened, which is the Book of Life. And the dead were judged according to their works, by the things which were written in the books. The sea gave up the dead who were in it, and Death and Hades delivered up the dead who were in them. And they were judged, each one according to his works. Then Death and Hades were cast into the lake of fire. This is the second death. And anyone not found written in the Book of Life was cast into the lake of fire," Rev 20:4-15.

From Rev20:4-15, it should be abundantly clear that the thousand-year Kingdom is nothing else but the Kingdom of God or Kingdom of Heaven. Although the duration of the reign of Christ is designated on the whole as a thousand years, we should understand this to signify an era immeasurable and undesignated. Therefore, its length is nothing else except the period between the First and Second Comings of the Lord, or more precisely, the period of the consolidation of the Kingdom of God until His Second Coming. This is the explanation of the Kingdom of God and its duration upon this earth.

As to the number 1000, it is always used as a symbol to the everlasting life with God which has no end. We must not forget that the Holy Bible tells us that "With the Lord one day is as a thousand years, and a thousand years as one day," 2Pt3:8. So the thousand-year reign is a symbol to the everlasting Kingdom of Christ: one unending day; the day of eternity. This is clear seeing that:

- In the period of this reign, the Devil was bound and loosed, receiving power over men. Christ entered into His dominion and bound the Devil, that is, by the redemption of humanity by His Blood He bound and restrained his power over mankind.

- The entrance into this Kingdom presupposes the first resurrection, that is, none other than Holy Baptism itself, often, in fact, called by the name of resurrection, or being born again from above or simply regeneration. This resurrection through Baptism is the first, in comparison to the second, the general one, of the body, which is also called the last resurrection, as when Martha spoke to Christ concerning her brother: "I know that he shall rise again at the resurrection on the Last Day," Jn11:24.

- At the end of this kingdom or reign, the Devil will again be let loose to deceive the people and with power and mania to assault and oppress holy Christians in the person of the antichrist, the beast or false prophet (Rev13:1-11).

- The duration of this period will be brief and yet it will constitute one of the signs signalling the immediacy of the Second Coming of Christ (Mt24:22; Rev13:5, 20:3).

Therefore, it should be clearly known that the first resurrection is the baptismal resurrection and the second resurrection is that which we wait for, on the last day, the last resurrection. Furthermore, it should also be clear that the first death is spiritual death that is consequence of sin. The second is the final death after the second resurrection. This second death is the torment eternal and apparently in hell (Mt18:8), so called due to its opposition to the blessed life of eternity (Jn5:24). It should also be clear that this second death has no power over those made worthy of the first resurrection.

"You were sealed with the Holy Spirit of promise, who is the guarantee of our inheritance until the redemption of the purchased possession, to the praise of His glory," Eph1:13-14. The Holy Spirit deposit is more than a hope, it is a guarantee involving this earth age, and the eternal to come. Consider in this context, that those 'dead in sin' are made alive again (or) born again, resurrected in truth into the 'new man', serving (or) reigning now in this earth age, and the age eternal to come.

"And I saw thrones, and they sat upon them, and judgment was given unto them: and [I saw] the souls of them that were beheaded for the witness of Jesus, and for the word of God, and which had not worshipped the beast, neither his image, neither had received [his] mark upon their foreheads, or in their hands; and they lived and reigned with Christ a thousand years. But the rest of the dead did not live again until the thousand years were finished. This is the first resurrection," Rev 20:4-5

LITERAL MILLENNIUM VIEW OF THE EARLY CHURCH

It is noteworthy to mention that the second "I saw" in Rev20:4 is not found in the original Greek. In addition, the Jews misinterpreted Rev20:5 to suit their hope for an earthly kingdom. We know that the Jews have their

>  There are two deaths and two resurrections. The first death is both the spiritual and physical death, which came from man's disobedience to the command of God, and the second death is eternal hell. By extension, the first resurrection is "those who are brought to life from dead works", which occurs through Baptism, Chrismation and the deadening of the passions, while the second resurrection is the alteration "from the corruption of the body to incorruption".
>
> — St Andrew of Caesarea

own materialistic thinking; they didn't accept Christ as their Lord because of His refusal of the earthly reign. Unfortunately, up to this day, they are still waiting for the Messiah who will have an earthly reign, and will give them dominion over the whole world.

This thinking was introduced into the Church in the beginning of its institution through the conversion of the Jews to Christianity, together with some of their materialistic imaginations. They diffused some of these

> There will be no coming of Jesus before His last appearance for judgment, for His coming is actually happening now in the Church and in her members. As for the first resurrection in the book of Revelation, it is metaphoric, and points to the interpretation of what happens to those who die in sin, then rise for a new life through repentance. So, the millennium has indeed begun, for Christ has conquered death and won on the cross, and now we His saints rule with Him, and through Him.
>
> — St Augustine

thoughts haphazardly among Church writings and sermons.

The school of Alexandria noticed the seriousness of the matter. St Origen opposed this idea of literal earthly kingdom. He was followed by Pope Dionysius the Alexandrian in the third century who refused the idea of the literal interpretation of the book of Revelation. Before the end of the fourth century this thought was on the point of vanishing completely in the Church of Alexandria. Abroad, St Augustine, after realizing his mistake, he clarified the danger of the literal interpretation of the millennium, giving strong proofs that it was wrong. And he considered he who proclaims it a heretic.

Premillennialists and Amillennialists have debated the nature of the "first resurrection" in Rev20:5 since the closure of the Holy Canon. Premillennialists insist that this "first resurrection" refers to the bodily resurrection of the Just at the time of the Second Coming of Christ while the Unjust will remain in the grave until a period of 1000 years of reign of Christ over the earth is completed. At that point, a "second resurrection", which will be only for sinners, will take place.

Amillennialists believe that such resurrection is not a reference to the bodily resurrection of the believers at the time of Christ's Second Coming, but to the resurrection of a soul dead in sins and trespasses to Life in Christ at the time of salvation.

The idea of the millennium appeared in some Protestant denominations. They made of it a principal belief, and started to set fixed dates for the coming of

Christ to reign a millennium. They proclaimed that first the Lord Jesus comes to reign over His saints before the coming of the "man of sin", and the occurrence of the great tribulation. Then He comes back once more to destroy the Antichrist. Secondly, Israel repents, but she remains a distinct body from the Church and Jerusalem gets wider, embellish herself, and becomes a centre for the Jewish people who will rule the world. Thirdly, there will come the rebuilding of the temple and the offering of animal sacrifices.

LITERAL EARTHLY MILLENNIUM REFUTED

Among the leaders of the Protestants, Erdmann thinks, that these principles on which the idea of the materialistic millennium is based, are contradictory to each other and is far from the spirit of the Holy Bible.

Ray Summers, in his book, "Worthy is the Lamb", thinks it is not appropriate to build a general skeleton comprising the last events, the divinity and the philosophy of history upon three verses (Rev20:4-6), in a literal insatiable interpretation.

H Monod refuses the literal interpretation of the

millennium as it was never mentioned in the Bible that the resurrection of the dead happens twice, or in two different periods. But it appears already in Is12:23, Jn5:5, 8:28, 1Th4:16-17, that the resurrection of the dead concerning the righteous and the wicked is followed immediately by judgment and eternal life.

H Monod, after debating the issue, comes out with this result: That Jesus Christ continues to reign, by enthroning His Bible within the person who accepts the Christian faith. In this way, Christianity will not be a tool at the governments' hand for politics. It will be a faithful expression of the way of life.

J Gable rejects the idea of the earthly millennium, by refuting the idea of the resurrection of the bodies to rule in a visual bodily kingdom. He says also, that the souls of the martyrs are alive, and they exercise a kind of resurrection as they taste a sort of rest, and a state of power and vitality. And somehow they practice authority with the Lord, for the amount of pain and trouble they bore at the time of their struggle for the Lord.

Obviously, these views attack violently the idea of the earthly millennium. The Jews' mistake is represented in their desire that the Messiah rules an earthly kingdom.

The Premillennialists fail to understand this true biblical doctrine due to a great extent to their materialistic mentality full of supposed "literalism" that looks forward for a kingdom of "earthly glory" and "national favouritism" which are completely contrary to Scripture. When we let the Bible speak on its own without "taking away" or "adding to" its meaning, then we can see how it all makes sense and becomes clear.

WHAT IS THE SECOND RESURRECTION?

The Lord Jesus tell us about it on more than one occasion, for instance: "For the hour is coming in which all who are in the graves will hear His voice and come forth — those who have done good, to the resurrection of life, and those who have done evil, to the resurrection of condemnation," Jn5:28-29. This means that the "second resurrection" takes place on Judgment Day at the Second Coming of Christ. For the righteous, it is everlasting life and inheritance of joy, glory, and light, while for the wicked, it is eternal death, or what is called the Second Death.

In summary, as Christians, we now live the "first

resurrection", every day of our lives after Baptism, dying to the love of the world, being liberated from its evil bondage, living by the power of the Resurrection of Christ in us, being steadfast in His commandments, witnessing to His love, and coming to fruition for the glory of His name. This is the "first resurrection". "Blessed and holy is he who has part in the first resurrection. Over such the second death has no power, but they shall be priests of God and of Christ, and shall reign with Him a thousand years," Rev20:6.

WHY NO CONDEMNATION NOW?

Why is there no longer any condemnatory judgment against us? The reason there is no condemnation has nothing to do with our somehow not deserving condemnation (we do), but with the fact that Our Lord Jesus bore the condemnation we deserved and as He is condemned no more, neither are we. We were judged guilty of breaking the Law (sin) but Sin has been judged in the propitiatory sacrifice and substitutionary atonement of Our Lord Jesus. Since Our Lord Jesus is not condemned by the Father, those who are in Him are not, will not, and cannot be condemned.

Christians are free from the "law of Sin and death",

which means, although they will commit sin, the Law no longer has the power to condemn them. We are not under the Law's condemnation because Our Lord Jesus fulfilled ("filled-up, completed") the expectations of the Law perfectly, and believers are "in Christ" (Rom8:3). St Paul also points out that genuine Christians, although they struggle, will not live "according to the flesh"; that is, they will not persist in a constant state of sinful living (Rom8:5). St Paul encourages us that we need not fear condemnation because we can come to God as our loving, forgiving Father (Rom8:15-16) and can retain the state of sanctity through repentance.

Believers are not only free from bondage to Sin; they are free from the inner emotions and thoughts that tend to bring feelings of condemnation to the Christian when he does commit sin (Rom8:2). How many Christians are filled with "guilt" because of trying to live up to some standard either self-imposed or placed up "over" you by another individual (this is legalism and it can be subtle). Believers can find solace in the assurance that we have been adopted into God's own family and have been made heirs of God and co-heirs with Christ (Rom8:17). Nothing can separate us "from the love of God that is in Christ Jesus" (Rom8:39).

 Christians who live in shame and guilt over past failures are needlessly condemning themselves when they ought to be "forgetting what is behind and straining toward what is ahead" (Php3:13). Fear can be paralysing, "but perfect love drives out fear" (1Jn4:18).

CONTRA UNIVERSALISM

Is St Paul a Universalist? If St Paul is a Universalist he would have said, "There is therefore now no condemnation to anyone! But he didn't. He said that only those in Christ, those walking according to the New Covenant, are not condemned. According to Universalists, everybody goes to heaven. Universalism is the teaching that God, through the atonement of Our Lord Jesus, will ultimately bring reconciliation between Himself and all people throughout history. This reconciliation will occur regardless of whether they have trusted in, or rejected, Our Lord Jesus as Saviour during their lifetime. The basic presuppositions of Universalism are that God is love and God loves everybody. They seem to focus on God's attribute of love. To say that God is love is the truth, but it is not the whole truth. Love is not God's only attribute; He has many others.

The Universalist also believes that God loves everybody, therefore, Christ died for everybody and, therefore, all will be saved. If God loves everyone, then it only makes sense that He will save everyone. God is the Saviour of all men who breathe air, live life, know healing in their human bodies because God is the sustainer of all of that. So, He is the Saviour of all, but especially does He sustain and provide for those who believe and will forever and ever do. And this is what St Paul is talking about in 1Ti4:10. St Paul is not a Universalist.

A Universalist writes: "Belief is not a 'requirement' to be returned back to God in spirit when you die. Belief is that thing that gives us joy right now, knowing that it has been accomplished, that the works of the Devil have been undone, and that Our Lord Jesus is the Saviour of the world." The Bible doesn't say that those who believe will have joy, but eternal life. To not believe is to not have eternal life: "He who is believing in the Son, has everlasting life; and he who does not believe the Son, shall not see life, but the wrath of God abides on him," Jn3:36.

The Scripture from beginning to end proclaims the

necessity of faith. Apart from faith in Christ men will perish. Eternal life is only for believers: "Christ has redeemed us from the curse of the Law, having become a curse for us (for it is written, "Cursed is everyone who hangs on a tree"), that the blessing of Abraham might come upon the Gentiles in Christ Jesus, that we might receive the promise of the Spirit through faith," Gal 3:13-14 quoting Dt21:23.

Our Lord Jesus received this curse, which we deserved and He did not, so that we could receive the blessing of Abraham, which He deserved and we did not! It would be enough if Our Lord Jesus simply took away the curse we deserved, but He did far more than that; He also gave a blessing that we didn't deserve! What is the blessing of Abraham? If the curse of the Law is death, what is the blessing? Life! The blessing of Abraham is eternal life. The parallelism of the two phrases in Gal 3:14 indicates that the blessing given to Abraham is equivalent to the promise of the Spirit.

Please notice what it is that the Gentiles (we) receive: "the promise of the Spirit". What is the promise of the Spirit? "And so, because he was a prophet, and knew that God had sworn to him with an oath to seat one of his descendants upon his throne, he looked ahead and spoke of the resurrection of the Christ, that His soul was not abandoned to Hades, nor did His flesh see corruption. This Jesus God raised up again, of which we are all witnesses. Therefore, having been exalted to the right hand of God, and having received from the Father the promise of the Holy Spirit, He has poured forth this which you both see and hear," Acts2:30-33.

The promise of the Spirit is the resurrection, which is life! "For the promise is for you and your children, and for all who are afar off, as many as the Lord our God shall call to Himself," Acts2:39. The promise that is to "as many as the Lord our God will call" is the promise of resurrection. And resurrection is life in the presence of God. To be under the curse is to be separated from God, and to be blessed is to be in His presence.

So how do we receive the promise? We would receive the promise of the Spirit through faith. St Paul doesn't say that everyone would receive the promise of the Spirit. The promise is received by faith. And only those who have faith receive it.

"But the Scripture has shut up everyone under sin, so that the promise by faith in Jesus Christ might be given to those who believe," Gal 3:22. Again the promise is given to, and only to, those who believe. "For you are all sons of God through faith in Christ Jesus," Gal 3:26. You become a son of God only through faith! "For God so loved the world that He gave His Only Begotten Son, that whoever believes in Him shall not perish, but have eternal life. For, God did not send the Son into the world to judge the world, but that the world might be saved through Him. He who believes in Him is not judged; he who does not believe has been judged already, because he has not believed in the name of the only begotten Son of God," Jn3:16-18. Notice that it is the one who believes that doesn't perish. It is the one who believes that is not judged.

The Scripture, foreseeing that God would justify the Gentiles by faith, preached the Gospel beforehand to Abraham, saying, "All the nations will be blessed in you," Gal 3:8-9. So then, those who are of faith are blessed with Abraham, the believer. It is only those who have faith that are blessed with Abraham, the Father of faith.

"And He Himself is the propitiation for our sins; and not for ours only, but also for those of the whole world,"

1Jn2:2. This is not teaching that Our Lord Jesus propitiates for everyone's sins, but that He is the only propitiation that there is. It is not speaking of universal propitiation, but of exclusiveness. In other words, there is no other propitiation other than Our Lord Jesus Christ. If they don't look to Christ, there is no one else to propitiate for their sins. Our Lord Jesus is the only propitiation for all the world (Acts4:10-12). So, 1Jn2:2 doesn't support Universalism either.

St Peter declared: "Let it be known to you all, and to all the people of Israel, that by the name of Jesus Christ of Nazareth, whom you crucified, whom God raised from the dead, by Him this man stands here before you whole. This is the 'stone which was rejected by you builders, which has become the chief cornerstone.' Nor is there salvation in any other, for there is no other name under heaven given among men by which we must be saved," Acts4:10-12.

The Universalist states that there is no unforgivable sin because all people who have ever lived will ultimately be reconciled to God. In other words, all sins from all people who have ever lived will be forgiven. However, the Bible teaches that there is a sin that will never be forgiven: blasphemy against the Spirit.

"Therefore I say to you, any sin and blasphemy shall be forgiven people, but blasphemy against the Spirit shall not be forgiven. Whoever speaks a word against the Son of Man, it shall be forgiven him; but whoever speaks against the Holy Spirit, it shall not be forgiven him, either in this age or in the age to come," Mt12:31-32.

In context of Mt12:31-32, the scribes had been given all of the evidence. They had seen the miracles. They had heard the teachings. And they still rejected Christ. They have just accused Him of performing miracles by the power of Satan. Our Lord Jesus was saying that it is the power of the Holy Spirit that is revealing who He is and what He came to do. The power of the Holy Spirit has made that so evident. The clear revelation of Christ as the

Messianic King, affirmed by the unmistakable healing and deliverance by the power of the Spirit, was totally rejected and declared to be of the devil. They attributed the work of God to Satan. They rejected the very One, Our Lord Jesus, in whom it was necessary to believe in order to receive forgiveness. As a result, there remained no possibility of forgiveness. So, if the unforgivable sin is to reject Our Lord Jesus Christ, then all who reject Him will perish.

The only unpardonable sin is to physically die having resisted the work of the Holy Spirit (Jn16:8-14) and rejected Our Lord Jesus as Saviour. Any sin today can be forgiven. But if they deny the person and work of Our Lord Jesus Christ, there is no means by which God can forgive them, because they have denied the only way to salvation. That's the unpardonable sin. The unpardonable sin is to deny Our Lord Jesus as the Christ. Every other sin can be forgiven. But to reject Our Lord Jesus Christ as the Saviour leaves no means by which God can grant forgiveness.

"Whoever speaks a word against the Son of Man, it shall be forgiven him; but whoever speaks against the Holy Spirit, it shall not be forgiven him, either in this age or in the age to come," Mt12:32. It shall not be forgiven him, either in this age or in the age to come. There are only two ages spoken of in the Bible and this sin won't be forgiven in either one of them. In the context of this passage men who were committing this sin, they would not be forgiven. They would not be saved: "Our Lord Jesus said to him, "I am the way, and the truth, and the life; no one comes to the Father, but through Me," Jn14:6. "The Lord is not slack concerning His promise, as some count slackness; but is longsuffering toward us, not willing that any should perish, but that all should come to repentance," 2Pt3:9. The "us" is referring to the elect, not all people.

Universalism has all men forgiven, the Bible does not. Why did St Paul and all the apostles sacrifice so much to preach the Gospel if it was really unnecessary because all men would be saved anyway. They were persecuted unto death, some were thrown into boiling caldrons of oil, some of them were burned at the stake, and some of them were crucified. Why go through all this to bring men the Gospel when all men will eventually be saved anyway?

"To the weak I became weak, that I might win the weak; I have become all things to all men, so that I may by all means save some," 1Co9:22. St Paul became all things to all men for the sake of bringing "some" to Christ. He also writes to St Timothy, "Remember Jesus Christ, risen from the dead, descendant of David, according to my Gospel, for which I suffer hardship even to imprisonment as a criminal; but the Word of God is not imprisoned. For this reason, I endure all things for the sake of those who are chosen, so that they also may obtain the salvation which is in Christ Jesus and with it eternal glory," 2Ti2:8-10.

So, what compels St Paul is not that he is responsible to save people, but that he has the high and holy privilege to be the instrument by which God saves people. So, his sufferings have an evangelistic purpose. The fact that God is using his preaching to save the elect enables him to endure anything. I'll say it again, St Paul was no Universalist, and neither am I.

God has chosen the elect to be saved, but God also gives us this incredible privilege of being the human agency by which the saving Gospel is brought to their hearts. They must believe, but they must hear so they can believe. That's the issue.

THE RESURRECTION OF THE DEAD

With death, the soul is separated from the body and remains separated until the Second Coming of Christ and the Final Judgement. What happens after the physical death?

AFTER DEATH

In the Hebrew Scriptures, the word used to describe the realm of the dead is Sheol. It simply means "the place of the dead" or "the place of departed souls/spirits." The New Testament Greek equivalent of Sheol is Hades, which also refers to "the place of the dead". The Orthodox Church believes in a post-death waiting period for departed souls, until the "Final Judgment", in one of two waiting places: "Paradise" for the good (Rev6:11) and "Hades" for the evil (2Pt2:9).

Sheol/Hades was a realm with two divisions — a place of blessing and a place of judgment (Mt11:23; 16:18; Lk10:15; 16:23; Acts2:27-31). The abodes of the saved and the lost are both generally called "Hades" in the Bible. The abode of the saved is also called "Abraham's bosom" (NKJV) or "Abraham's side" (NIV) in Lk16:22 and "Paradise" in Lk23:43. The abode of the unsaved is called

"Hell" (NKJV) or "Hades" (NIV) in Lk16:23. The abodes of the saved and the lost are separated by a "great chasm" (Lk16:26). When Jesus died, He went to the blessed side of Sheol (1Pt3:18-20) and, from there, took the believers with Him to heaven (Eph4:8-10). The judgment side of Sheol/Hades has remained unchanged. All unbelieving dead go there awaiting their Final Judgment in the future.

When the saints of God leave this world, their spirits are immediately ushered into the presence of the Lord. This was the conviction St Paul held. "We are confident, I say, and willing rather to be absent from the body, and to be present with the Lord," 2Co5:8. "For I am hard-pressed between the two, having a desire to depart, and to be with Christ; which is far better," Php1:23. Presently, for all those who left this world in a saved condition and in a state of Grace, their souls are in the presence of the Lord Jesus Christ. St Paul also said, "Imitate me as I also imitate Christ," 1Co11:1. On the Cross, Our Lord Jesus Christ promised the penitent thief after pronouncing his faith in Jesus, "Assuredly I say to you, today you will be with Me in Paradise," Lk23:43. There are no "wandering souls", or "roaming souls".

Hell (or Gehenna) is a term used to refer to the condition of everlasting separation from God in eternity. It is the condition of Satan and his angels and will be the condition of those who rejected Christ in this life (2Pt2:9). Rev20:11-15 gives a clear distinction between Hades and the lake of fire (Hell). The lake of fire is the permanent and final place of judgment for the lost. Hades, then, is a temporary place. Many people refer to both Hades and the lake of fire as hell, and this causes confusion.

Therefore, after death, a person resides in a "temporary" heaven or hell. After this temporary realm, at the final resurrection, a person's eternal destiny will not change. The precise location of that eternal destiny is what changes. Believers will ultimately be granted entrance into the new heavens and new earth (Rev21:1). Unbelievers will ultimately be sent to the lake of fire (Rev20:11-15). These are the final, eternal destinations of all people — based entirely on whether or not they had trusted Jesus Christ alone for salvation (Mt25:46; Jn3:36).

SLEEPING OF SOULS, PRIVATE JUDGMENT AND PURGATORY
Some religions and Christian denominations however, advocate such concepts as "sleeping of souls", "private judgment" and the "purgatory", some or all of which are

claimed to occur between a person's death and the "General Judgment". The Orthodox Church does not condone these beliefs. The arguments regularly advanced in support of some kind of a purgatory, however modernized, do not come from the Bible. They come from the common perception that all of us up to the time of death are still sinful, and from the proper assumption that something needs to be done about this if we are (to put it crudely) to be at ease in the presence of the holy and sovereign God. The medieval doctrine of purgatory imagined that the 'something' that needed to be done could be divided into two aspects: punishment on the one hand, and purging or cleansing on the other.

It is vital that we understand the biblical response to both of these concepts. I cannot stress sufficiently that punishment for sin has already been dealt with on the Cross of Jesus. The idea that Christians need to suffer punishment for their sins in a post-mortem purgatory, or anywhere else, reveals a straightforward failure to grasp the very heart of what was achieved on the cross. In the New Testament, bodily death itself actually puts sin to an end. There may well be all kinds of sins still lingering on within us, infecting us and dragging us down. But part of the biblical understanding of death, bodily death, is that it finishes all that off at a single go.

Christians are assured that their sins have already been dealt with through the death of Christ; they are now no longer under threat because of them. First, there is faith and baptism. "You are already made clean", says Jesus, "by the Word which I have spoken to you," Jn15.3. The Word of the Gospel, awakening faith in the heart, is itself the basic cleansing that we require. "The one who has washed", said Jesus at the supper, "doesn't need to wash again, except for his feet; he is clean all over," Jn13.10. The "feet" here seem to be representing the part of us which still, so to speak, stands on the muddy ground of this world. This is where "the sin which so easily gets in the way" (Heb12.1) finds, we may suppose, its opportunity. By repentance we continue to be cleansed through the Blood of Christ.

The Holy Bible's position is clearly against these, as shown, for example, in the parable of Lazarus the beggar, and the rich man (Lk16:19-31). In this parable, there is no mention of either "purgatory" or "sleeping souls". The "great gulf" is not a geographical divide, but the complete separation between virtue and wickedness, a separation that cannot be overcome after death. Note that torments have not changed the rich man's heart, as he still sees Lazarus as a servant existing for his own comfort. In addition, the torment he is experiencing would be a foretaste of his final state. Jesus plainly used this story to teach that after death the unrighteous are eternally separated from God, that they remember their rejection of the Gospel, that they are in torment, and that their condition cannot be remedied.

However, the souls of the departed, while in the waiting place and having got rid of the body, continue to feel the conditions of the living: a man, not even a believer, calls out from Hades and converses with St Abraham! The intercessions of a wicked man are heard, but avail nothing. In contrast, "the effective, fervent prayer of a righteous man avails much," Jam5:16.

The ignorance of Scripture is a great cliff and a deep abyss. It is impossible for anyone to be without benefit if he reads continually and with attention.

— St John Chrysostom

> This life has been given to you for repentance; do not waste it in vain pursuits.
>
> – St Isaac of Syria

For the Orthodox Christian, however, a proper understanding of the future life is essential to living in a God-pleasing, joyous, and fulfilled manner on earth. Orthodox understand that Hell is a choice; that a person's view of the future determines how he or she lives in the present.

> Meditation upon one's own death and the Judgment that awaits him is not something that promotes morbid introspection, but rather the true repentance that leads to the fullness of life and joy in Christ. May this soon be your discovery as well.

The Resurrection Of The Dead

THE DOCTRINE OF THE SECOND COMING

"This Jesus who was taken up from you into heaven, will come the same way as you saw Him go into heaven," Acts1:11. These words of the angels are addressed to the apostles at the ascension of the Lord. Christ will come again in glory, "not to deal with sin, but to save those who are eagerly waiting for Him" (Heb9:28).

The coming of the Lord at the end of the ages will be the Day of Judgment which is the Day of the Lord foretold in the Old Testament and predicted by Jesus Himself (e.g. Daniel 7; Matthew 24). The exact time of the end is not foretold, not even by Jesus, so that men would always be prepared by constant vigil and good works.

The very presence of Christ as the Truth and the Light is itself the judgment of the world. In this sense, all men and the whole world are already judged or, more accurately, already live in the full presence of that reality — Christ and His works — by which they will be ultimately judged. With Christ now revealed, there is no longer any excuse for ignorance and sin (Jn9:39).

At this point it is necessary to note that at the Final Judgment there will be those "on the left hand" who will go into "the eternal fire prepared for the devil and his angels" (Mt25:41; Rev20). That this is the case is no fault of God's. It is the fault only of men, for the Lord says: "as I hear, I judge and My judgment is just," Jn5:30.

"For the Lord Himself will descend from heaven with a cry of command, with the archangels' call, and with the sound of the trumpet of God. And the dead in Christ will rise first; then we who are alive, who are left, shall be caught up in the cloud to meet the Lord in the air, and so we shall always be with the Lord," 1Th4:16-17.

THE DOCTRINE OF ETERNAL HELL
In Lk16:19-31, Jesus clearly taught the existence of heaven and hell. God takes no "pleasure in the death of the wicked" (Ezk18:22). He "desires all men to be saved and to come to the knowledge of the Truth" (1Ti2.4). He does everything in His power so that salvation and eternal life would be available and possible for all. There is nothing more that God can do. Everything now depends on man.

If some men refuse the gift of life in communion with God, the Lord can only honour this refusal and respect the freedom of His creatures which He Himself has given and will not take back. God allows men to live "with the devil and his angels" if they so desire. Even in this He is loving and just. For if God's presence as the "consuming fire" (Heb12.29) and the "unapproachable light" (1Ti6.16) which delight those who love Him only produce hatred and anguish in those who do not "love His appearing" (2Ti4.8), there is nothing that God can do except either to destroy His sinful creatures completely, or to destroy Himself. But God will exist and will allow His creatures to exist. He also will not hide His Face forever.

The doctrine of eternal hell, therefore, does not mean that God actively tortures people by some unloving and perverse means. It does not mean that God takes delight in the punishment and pain of His people whom He loves. Neither does it mean that God "separates Himself" from His people, thus causing them anguish in this separation (for indeed if people hate God, separation would be welcome, and not abhorred!). It means rather that God continues to allow all people, saints and sinners alike, to exist forever. All are raised from the dead into everlasting life: "those who have done good, to the resurrection of life, and those who have done evil, to the resurrection of judgment," Jn5:29. In the end, God will be "all and in all" (1Co15.28). For those who love God, resurrection from the dead and the presence of God will be Paradise. For those who hate God, resurrection from the dead and the presence of God will be Hell. This is the teaching of the Fathers of the Church.

 There is sprung up a light for the righteous, and its partner is joyful gladness. And the light of the righteous is everlasting....

One light alone let us shun — that which is the offspring of the sorrowful fire....

For I know a cleansing fire which Christ came to send upon the earth, and He Himself is called a Fire. This Fire takes away whatsoever is material and of evil quality; and this He desires to kindle with all speed....

I know also a fire which is not cleansing, but avenging.... which He pours down on all sinners.... that which is prepared for the devil and his angels.... that which proceeds from the Face of the Lord and shall burn up His enemies round about.... the unquenchable fire which is eternal for the wicked. For all these belong to the destroying power, though some may prefer even in this place to take a more merciful view of this fire, worthily of Him who chastises.

– St Gregory the Theologian

Those who find themselves in Gehenna will be chastised with the scourge of love. How cruel and bitter this torment of love will be! For those who understand that they have sinned against Love undergo greater sufferings than those produced of the most fearful tortures. The sorrow which takes hold of the heart which has sinned against Love is more piercing than any other pain. It is not right to say that sinners in hell are deprived of the love of God. But Love acts in two different ways, as suffering in the reproved, and as joy in the blessed.

– St Isaac of Syria

Thus, man's final judgment and eternal destiny depends solely on whether or not man loves God and His brethren. It depends on whether or not man loves the light more than the darkness — or the darkness more than the light. It depends, we might say, on whether or not man loves Love and Light Itself; whether or not man loves Life — which is God Himself; the God who is revealed in creation, in all things, and in the "least of the brethren."

The conditions of the Final Judgment are already known. Christ has given them Himself with absolute clarity (Mt25:31-46; Rom2:6-13).

"The hour is coming when all who are in the tombs will hear His voice and come forth, those who have done good, to the resurrection of life, and those who have done evil, to the resurrection of judgement," Jn5:28-29.

At the Final Judgement, man will be presented before Christ as a full person, with a body and soul. For man to be presented like this, his body must be resurrected and be united with the soul. This will happen immediately before the Final Judgement. The Holy Scripture absolutely assures us of this. Let us see some of its passages.

"Lo! I tell you a mystery. We shall not all sleep, but we shall all be changed, in a moment, in the twinkling of an eye, at the last trumpet. For the trumpet will sound, and the dead will be raised imperishable, and we shall be changed," 1Col5:51-52.

"For since we believe that Jesus died and rose again, even so, through Jesus, God will bring with Him those who have fallen asleep. For this we declare to you by the word of the Lord, that we who are alive, who are left until the coming of the Lord, shall not precede those who have fallen asleep. For the Lord himself will descend from heaven with a cry of command, with the archangel's call, and with the sound of the

trumpet of God. And the dead in Christ will rise first; then we who are alive, who are left, shall be caught up together with them in the clouds to meet the Lord in the air; and so, we shall always be with the Lord," 1Th4:14-17.

From the above passages of the Holy Scripture, we are clearly taught beyond any doubt that:

• The dead will be resurrected before the Second Coming of Christ and Final Judgement. "All who are in the tombs shall hear His voice, and come forth," Jn5:28.

• The resurrected body will be immortal. "The dead will be raised imperishable" (1Co15:52).

• Before the Second Coming or during it, the living will be changed; in other words, their bodies, like those of the dead, will be spiritualized and made immortal: "The dead will be raised imperishable, and we shall be changed," 1Co15:52.

• The living and the dead will proceed to eternal life or eternal hell. "And come forth, those who have done good, to the resurrection of life, and those who have done evil, to the resurrection of judgment," Jn5:29.

With the resurrection of the dead and the Final Judgement, death is abolished. The end of the world also comes, but this does not mean the catastrophic end to the world but rather change and finality. Sin will disappear.

Thrice-Holy God, Who with Your infinite love created and continue to sustain us, You admire and bless us whenever we do good, You tolerate us when we sin, You forgive us when we repent. You deigned that Your only begotten Son should become man, to be crucified, to die as a man, to be resurrected and become the first-born from the dead, and to make possible our own resurrection. We thank You for all these things. We ask You please to give us repentance. Make it so that we will proceed to the resurrection of life and not to judgement. Grant us eternal life. Do not allow our eternal punishment. Do not deprive us of the joy of Your everlasting presence.

THE GREAT WHITE THRONE JUDGEMENT

When Christ takes His seat to judge the living and the dead, the earth and the sky "flee" from His presence (Rev20:11). Obviously, this seat exists beyond the confines of "the heavens and the earth" mentioned in Gn1:1. Living beings, angels and humans, remain alive in place beyond the "very good" Earth. Some go to the place of "second death" (Rev20:14) and some remain in the glorious presence of God. At this point, God has no more use for this planet and cosmos. The new creation will be filled with "light" without any darkness or shadows and without such entities as the sun, stars, and light bulbs as sources of illumination (Rev21:23, 22:4).

Many Bible scholars view Eccl3:14, "I know that everything God does will endure forever; nothing can be added to it and nothing taken from it" and Heb4:3, "(God's) work has been finished since the creation of the world" as declarations of God's sovereign, immutable plan for humanity. In other words, God's has determined what He will do and nothing can change that. As for Dan12:3, "(Those) who led many to righteousness (will shine) like the stars for ever and ever", the shining "forever" seems in the context of the larger passage to describe "those who lead many to righteousness".

God has promised to His believers a reward far beyond what anyone, no matter how spiritual or imaginative, can conceive. Moreover, the doctrine of heaven is one of the chief distinctions between Christianity and other belief systems. Many cults, for example Islam, promise an earth-bound (or planet-bound) paradise replete with physical pleasures, including sexual pleasure. Christianity promises deliverance from earthly paradise, no matter how magnificently restored its condition.

The Doctrine of the Second Coming teaches us to maintain a constant state of watchfulness and purity to enjoy the glory of the eternal life. The Doctrine of the Second Coming is called in Greek "Eschatology". It is the last stage in God's plan of Grace, which composes four stages: Preparation (for Jesus' First Coming), Justification (by faith in Jesus' saving death on the Cross), Sanctification (by the Holy Spirit) and Glorification (at Jesus' Second Coming).

Our belief in the Second Coming is documented in the Nicene Creed: "And He shall come again in His glory to judge the living and the dead, whose kingdom shall have no end…We look for the resurrection of the dead and the life of the coming age."

WE GROAN IN HOPE

"For we know that the whole creation groans and labours with birth pangs together until now. And not only they, but we also who have the firstfruits of the Spirit, even we ourselves groan within ourselves, eagerly waiting for the adoption, the redemption of our body?!" Rom8:22-23. Such is the condition of the creation that has been brought into existence for our sakes. How much more should we moan and labour too in order to enjoy the fullness of the glory of God's adopted children!

WE HOPE FOR SONSHIP

Heart change comes quickly on the heels of Salvation. This is because at Baptism our entire being and nature is completely changed and at Confirmation we get the Holy Spirit deposited inside of us testifying to the fact that we now belong to the family of God. The Holy Spirit is given to us as the firstfruits of our eternal redemption through Christ Our Lord Jesus. This is a foretaste of the blissful things that are to come. Our bodies long to be clothed with Christ and like the other creation, we groan inwardly and wait for this adoption to take place.

The Father's desire is not merely to produce babes in Christ; He is also looking for mature sons who will bring

His glory to a needy world. There is a birthing process to reveal the character of Our Lord Jesus through His mature sons to all of creation. The life of Christ is formed in us through "travail", and travail involves suffering and sorrow. So, this is why St Paul mentions that "our present sufferings are not worth comparing with the glory that will be revealed in us" (Rom8:18). That travail will bring forth that glory. The concept of giving birth to Christ's life in a spiritual sense is a glorious hope set before us. It refers to a level of spiritual maturity where we become channels through which the fullness of His life flows to others. This is a theme that is repeated many times throughout the Bible. This is why the Bible refers so often to travail, intercession, and giving birth.

St Paul wrote, "We who have the firstfruits of the Spirit groan within ourselves, eagerly waiting for the adoption (Sonship), the redemption of our body," Rom8:23. Here, St Paul links the placing of the mature sons of God with the resurrection of our bodies. In Php3:10-12, St Paul links the maturity of the saints or "being perfected" with the resurrection, where he rejoices in the sufferings of Christ that he may "attain to the resurrection from the dead." So, the goal of the maturing Christian is to be engaged in the struggle of faith, confident that Christ has made us His own, but knowing that we are not yet perfected. We will now see that labouring and sorrow is required before this "revealing" of God's character and glory will take place. But like St Paul, we should "consider that the sufferings of this present time are not worthy to be compared with the glory which shall be (future tense) revealed in us" (Rom8:18). Christ in us is our Only Hope of Glory! (Col 1:27). This means that "salvation" is past, when we first put our faith in Christ, present, as we continue in the struggle of faith, and future, when we will receive the redemption of our body.

"For we know that the whole creation groans and labours with birth pangs together until now. And not only they, but we also who have the firstfruits of the Spirit, even we ourselves groan within ourselves, eagerly waiting for the adoption, the redemption of our body," Rom8:22-23.

These firstfruits (Rom8:23) appeared in the age of the apostle Paul when the apostles could exorcise demons and raise the dead through the casting of their shadow (Acts5:15), and their clothes (Acts19:12). These are the firstfruits, so what would the fullness of the Spirit be? Therefore, let us expect the fullness of the glory of adoption by the resurrection of the body from the dead. Accordingly, what we have received as the firstfruits of the Spirit opens the door of hope. In this manner man is motivated to patiently struggle through humility and brokenness until he attains the fullness of the Spirit. It is He who glorifies the whole of man, soul and body, on an eternal level.

"Not only that, but we also who have the firstfruits of the Spirit, even we ourselves waiting for the adoption, the redemption of our body," Rom8:23. Though we have so much of heaven already within us, we groan within ourselves waiting for the adoption, not (be it observed) the deliverance of ourselves from the body, but the redemption of the body itself from the grave. The word "adoption" is used five times in the New Testament (Rom8:15, 23, 9:4; Gal 4:5; and Eph1:5). People draw many analogies from this term that have merit, but this verse makes it very clear that the term "adoption" is referring to the time when we will receive our glorified bodies.

>  The firstfruits of the Spirit which we have received, urge us to this inner moaning which is filled with hope. These firstfruits are tremendously great and do not end with the Spirit forgiving our sins, for they also grant us righteousness and sanctification.
>
> – St John Chrysostom

WE HOPE FOR THE REDEMPTION OF OUR BODIES

The Holy Spirit is called the "firstfruits" of our salvation. Where there are first fruits, there has to be further fruit. St Paul spoke of the Holy Spirit as being the earnest, or down payment, of our salvation with more to come (2Co5:5 and Eph1:14). As wonderful as our salvation is right here in this life, it is not complete. The flesh (Rom7:18) is a constant source of trouble, and even victorious Christians groan for the time when we will be delivered from this flesh at the redemption of our bodies (2Co5:1-4). And even we Christians, although we have the Holy Spirit within us as a foretaste of future glory, also groan to be released from pain and suffering. We, too, wait anxiously for that day when

God will give us our full rights as His children, including the new bodies He has promised us.

The English word "redemption" was translated from the Greek word "apolutrosis" and this Greek word means "(the act of paying) ransom in full" (Strong's Concordance). However, it is specifying more than just the payment of a ransom; it includes the deliverance that comes as a result (Vine's Expository Dictionary). So, St Paul was speaking of the time when we will experience in our bodies what Our Lord Jesus has already purchased for us. This can be illustrated by the way trading stamps are used. First, the stamps have to be purchased, and then they are redeemed for the desired product. The purchase is essential, but so is the redemption. No one really wants the stamps. They want what the stamps can be redeemed for.

Our Lord Jesus purchased redemption for us – spirit, soul, and body – but our redemption is not completed yet. Our spirits are the only part of us that have experienced total redemption (Mt26:41). The purchase for our total salvation has already been made with the blood of Our Lord Jesus, but our bodies are not redeemed yet. That is to say, we have not yet received all the benefits of that transaction in our physical bodies. That will take place at the Second Coming of the Lord, when we receive our new glorified bodies.

The terms "adoption," "redemption," must here be taken in a restricted sense. Our present adoption into God's family is as perfect as God can make it. We shall not in reality be more the children of God in heaven than we are now. "Beloved, now are we the sons of God", and all the immunities and blessings of a present sonship are ours. Equally as complete is our redemption from all that can condemn. When Our Lord Jesus exclaimed, "It is finished!" by one offering He perfected forever the salvation of His Church.

On this earth, we long and groan under the burden of this body because we are being fitted with a heavenly body fashioned after Our Lord Jesus (2Co5:2-5). But in the same way that He is preparing us and making us fit for this heavenly body, the Holy Spirit is given to us as a guarantee of the fulfilment of this promise while on this earth (2Co5:5). So, in this we can rejoice knowing that we have already received the firstfruits of our redemption.

In 2 Corinthians 5, St Paul talks about an inward groaning in which we long to be further clothed and fitted with our heavenly dwelling. The Spirit of God has brought us into new relationships. He has given us the spirit of adoption towards the Father. He has made us to feel our brotherhood with the saints, and to know our union with Christ. We are not in our relationships what we used to be, for we were "heirs of wrath even as others". But now we are "heirs of God, joint heirs with Our Lord Jesus Christ". Consequently, we cannot help loving, for love alone could make the new relation to be fully enjoyed.

The corruptible body weighs down the soul, and the earthly body pulls down a mind full of cares. For as soon as the Spirit comes to dwell in us and turns us to the study of virtue, the love of the flesh jumps up to combat it and the law in our members which is prone to silly lusts, begins a bitter struggle. That is why we groan waiting for the liberation of our bodies as a result of the adoption.

— St John Chrysostom

The blessed Spirit has also brought us under new obligations. We were bound to love God and serve Him as creatures, but we did not do it: now the Holy Spirit has made us to feel that we are debtors to infinite love and mercy through redemption. Every drop of Our Lord Jesus' blood cries to us to love. The love of Christ constrains us: we must love, for the Spirit has taken of the things of the loving Christ and has revealed them unto us (Jn16:14).

For we were saved in this hope, but hope that is seen is not hope; for why does one still hope for what he sees? But if we hope for what we do not see, we eagerly wait for it with perseverance," Rom8:24-25.

WE HOPE FOR COMPLETE SALVATION
The Apostle continues his discourse on hope and on attaining fullness of the Spirit in Rom8:24-25. Hope is a Grace of the Holy Spirit, produced by Him in the believer, and drawn forth into act and exercise by the promises of the Word. It is made up of desire and expectation. Its object is something good, for we cannot desire evil; nor is

hope the right word, when evil is the object. It must be good, or what appears to be good.

Hope is a future thing, for we do not desire or expect that which is present or possessed. It is unseen, hidden in God, laid up for us in heaven, reserved against that day. Hope is the child of faith, which faith is the confident expectation of things hoped for, the full persuasion of things not seen (Heb11:1). We cannot hope for what we do not believe, or expect but as we believe God's promises.

The highest object of our hope is complete salvation, called "the hope that is laid up for us in heaven", even the full possession of God's glorious salvation, which is ready to be revealed in the last time. Hope is founded on the covenant of Grace, as it includes the gifts and promises of the Father, and the offices and engagements of the Son. Surely our hope finds a firm, a settled, and an immovable foundation! Hope, or the strongest desire for the greatest good, and a lively expectation of the most glorious blessings, is warranted, fully warranted in God's most holy Word, and becomes at once one of our greatest privileges, and a most solemn duty.

WE HOLD ON TO HOPE

"We are saved by hope", not in the same sense as we are saved by faith, which delivers us from guilt, degradation, and eternal death, by receiving from Christ, and confiding in Christ. To be saved by hope is to be kept, preserved, upheld, or sustained, in the midst of foes, dangers, and trials. Hope quickens us in duties and preserves us from becoming cold and dead. It comforts us in tribulations and keeps us from being disheartened and gloomy. It enables us to overcome temptation and so to hold on our way, looking unto Our Lord Jesus. It gives us peace in death in the sure prospect of victory over the grave. Thus, hope saves us:

- By preventing despair into which we can never fall while hope lives within us;
- By preserving us from desperation — to the verge of which we are sometimes brought;
- By guarding us against rebellion — the seeds of which are still thickly sown in our corrupt hearts; and
- By protecting us against apostasy — into which we can never fall so long as we hope in God.

Hope always generates patience, therefore we read of the "patience of hope in Our Lord Jesus Christ". The stronger our hope, the steadier is our patience; and the steadier our patience, the more unruffled is our peace. Salvation includes our election which is past, our effectual calling and sanctification which are present, and our glorification which is future. We were chosen to salvation by the Father; we are redeemed by Our Lord Jesus Christ; we are sanctified by the Holy Spirit. We shall be glorified by the cooperation, and as the joint work, of the whole of the Divine Persons in the Godhead.

Hope is in God as its highest object and best end. Hope is through Christ who is the way to the Father, the truth, and the life. Hope is on the ground of the Word, which warrants, excites, and regulates it. Hope is for all that God has promised, whether temporal or spiritual, in this world or the next.

O God of hope, we beseech You to fill us with all joy and peace in believing, that we may abound in hope, by the power of the Holy Spirit.
Lord Jesus, You are our hope: as such be ever present with us, unfolding Your glory before us, and imparting more and more of Your Spirit unto us.

Holy Spirit, fill us with a lively hope, and teach us to expect all that God has promised, all that Christ has procured, and all that You have revealed in Your Most Holy Word.

The firstfruits of the Spirit motivates us to hold on to hope in order to attain the full glory which the Spirit grants to the children of God. However, this hope does not take root through negative behaviour. In other words, a believer needs to play a positive role by tolerating many hardships and pain on account of his hope in intangible matters. That is why the Apostle says: "...we eagerly wait for it with perseverance" (Rom8:25).

So that you may know that you do not stand alone facing the struggles and dangers, but that divine Grace stands beside you. Even in matters that are completely easy, He works with you, and He plays a role in His union with you under all circumstances.

– St John Chrysostom

hope that is seen is not hope; for why does one still hope for what he sees? But if we hope for that we do not see, we eagerly wait for it with perseverance," Rom8:24, 25. It is very clear that hope is not based on what is seen. Someone who says, "I have no reason to hope," doesn't understand what hope is. Hope comes directly from God (Rom15:13) through His Word (Rom15:4). Hope is more than wishful thinking, more than optimism. It is settled confidence concerning things to come. Hope produces patience. When we are in need of patience, we are in need of hope (Rom5:3). This hope is so sure that we can patiently endure suffering in anticipation of Christ's Kingdom.

THE OVERCOMING KING

"The voice of my beloved! Behold, he comes leaping upon the mountains, skipping upon the hills. My beloved is like a gazelle or a young stag," SS2:8-9a.

Our natural tendency is self-centeredness, maintaining the status quo and living life out of a sense of merely following duty and obligation. We need to hear the call of our Lord to venture forth so that we can be stretched by the exercise of faith once again. The Spirit solemnly charged others to not disturb her as she sat at the Wedding Table under the apple tree. "I charge you...do not stir up (disturb) nor awaken love until He pleases," SS2:7. However, the Lord is now disturbing her as the season in her life suddenly changes.

This passage marks the beginning of a significant turning in the Bride's life. The Bride is experiencing a new dimension of the King. Jesus reveals Himself to her as the sovereign King over the nations who effortlessly conquer all the difficult mountains or high places. She sees Jesus as a gazelle or a young stag (adult male deer) that may easily leap in victory on the mountains. A gazelle or young stag has the ability to easily and quickly ascend a mountain with boundless energy.

The Word Incarnate, who came in the fullness of time (many years after the fall of man), was not slow to save us. He came to prepare salvation. In the fullness of time,

He descended to us before we even began to seek Him. The Bridegroom did not ask for the easy road but swiftly and joyfully accepted to suffer for our sake. "Looking unto Jesus the author and finisher of our faith, who for the joy that was set before Him endured the Cross, despising the shame...," Heb12:2.

The swiftness of the gazelle or the young stag leaping upon the mountains pictures not only the vitality of youth and adventure, but is a perfect symbol of the abundant life Jesus offers all who follow Him. This is the third revelation of Jesus in the Song. She only knew Jesus as the Counselling Shepherd (SS1:7-11) and the Affectionate Father (SS1:12) sitting at the table feeding her grapes and apples with love. Now she sees a different aspect of His personality; she sees Him as the Overcoming One who is victorious over the mountains (obstacles, fears, trials) of life. The deer also runs toward the brooks of water. On the way, he kills the serpents and becomes thirstier for the water brooks. David said, "As the deer pants for the water brooks, so pants my soul for you, O God," Ps42:1. The Son of God came as a deer thirsty for our love. Along the path of salvation, because of His love to us, He destroyed the old serpent (Satan).

King Jesus triumphed over all demonic powers and principalities (Eph1:22). He has overcome all obstacles (human and demonic). We command the "mountains of adversity" to move. The hills being smaller than mountains speak of the smaller difficulties we face. "For assuredly, I say to you, whoever says to this mountain, 'Be removed and be cast into the sea,' and does not doubt in his heart... those things he says will be done...," Mk11:23. Zerubbabel was to speak grace to the mountains of adversity that stood before him. "Who are you, O great mountain? Before Zerubbabel you shall become a plain! And he shall bring forth the capstone with shouts of 'Grace, grace to it!'" Zec4:7.

Jesus is asking the Bride to step out in faith, trust His love and follow Him in victory over the trials of life.

The Bride has been in a place of comfort (under the apple tree) and the King calls her to "arise" and begin to climb mountains with Him. He is challenging her to come higher with Him, but it is not easy; mountains are difficult to climb. She recognizes the voice of her Beloved, the One who she loves.

"Behold, he stands behind our wall; he is looking through the windows, gazing through the lattice," SS2:9b. Jesus speaks tenderly to us in love when He calls us out of the comfort zone to join Him on the dangerous mountains of risk. Jesus is pictured as standing or as ready for action. He is usually pictured in Scripture as sitting in rest and victory with His feet upon His enemies (Ps110:1). When Stephen died, the Lord stood up to receive him (Acts7:55). When He stands, powerful things are about to happen.

Jesus stands behind a wall looking into the house in which the Bride sits undisturbed. Jesus is described as standing outside the door of the Laodicean church as He knocked (Rev3:20). She rightly describes it as "our" wall. It is not her wall but their wall because she had been led by the Spirit's commission to remain undisturbed at the Table until He awakened her (SS2:7). The wall stands for the believer's separation from the world. The King emphasizes that NOW (SS2:11-14) is the time to come with Him and conquer the things He is focused on. The King is responding to the Bride's request (SS1:4) to be drawn after Him. He is drawing her into oneness and in ministry. God's life is always new, there is always more of Him, the revelation of His dimensions can and will go on forever; it's the glory of God!

The Bride has been in a place of isolation in a real focused way for a season. The Spirit mandated that no one disturb her in the verse just before in SS2:7. It was a result of her obedience to the Holy Spirit that she finds herself behind a wall; it was a wall of protection, and the Lord hemmed her in. Sometimes the Lord calls people to that season for an extended period of time like Moses in the wilderness for forty years; St John the Baptist, his entire life until He was thirty years old; David was there for seven years; he was not ruling as king. He was in the wilderness and before that as a boy just singing his love songs to God.

We are creatures of habit, falling easily into comfortable routines. Shulamite speaks of "our wall" indicating she wants to have her safe, protected, sheltered private relationship with God. The words "window" and "lattice" are plural in Hebrew. Jesus looks at her through the windows with the intention of wooing her with His gaze to draw her forth into a deeper relationship with Himself. The wall of separation from the world has also become a wall insulating her from the hurts and pains of the world. God is very much involved in the world, and He does so in fresh new ways. Either we respond to His call and venture forth with

Him, or we shall be left out altogether.

"My beloved speaks and says to me: 'Arise, my love, my fair one, and come away'," **SS2:10**. Now, He speaks to her and He says to her, "My Beloved" (SS2:10). He is speaking tenderly. He says: "Come with Me back to the mountain tops. We are going to leave the house where you are walled in in the safety zone, the comfort zone and you are going to go with Me. You are going to follow Me to the mountains of faith and obedience, to costly obedience and to that risky, even difficult assignment where you do not have certainty like you had in the season before. You might not end up looking good. You might not end up with honour in the new season. You might end up in a whole different place, but you are dear to God and His eyes are upon you".

Jesus challenges us to the mountains of total faith and obedience. These high places involve embracing difficult assignments and relationships that challenge our sense of security and comfort. She does not like the risk and heights of the mountains, but only wants to sit under the shade tree eating apples with Jesus (SS2:3). The question is, is it safe to go with Jesus out of the comfort zone? Is it safe? Is it good? Will you have life at the heart level, if you obey the Lord one hundred percent?

If Jesus is on the water, is it safer in the water, than it is the boat? It is safer to be on the water: St Peter was in the boat, and he got out of the boat, and he walked on the water. It is safer on the water with Jesus than it is in the boat without Him. Many people are committed to the boat, their knuckles are white, and they are hanging on the boat. If Jesus is not in the boat, the boat is not safe. In the flesh, it seems safer to be in the boat without Jesus instead of being on the water with Him. You want to be safe in the Will of God where Jesus is.

We find our safety in God's Grace in two places, the cleft and the cliff. She must rise if she is to experience mature partnership with Jesus. This is one of the most practical foundational truths that all of us must live in. We would like a contract with the Lord. 'Lord, I will obey in the next season, but I want to make sure that circumstances will be better'. Many people make all of their life choices based on circumstances becoming better. That is the only grid they have. They have no grid of going to a mountain of risk. Many believers do, and many do not. So, they would like to make a contract with the Lord, I will obey in this next season, but I would like some kind of certainty that I will have more honour, a little bit more comfort, and a little bit more money.

Well, I tell you that His banner over you is to bring you to the experience of love and not necessarily to make your life easy. He says, "Come to the mountain top". Sometimes, it does result in more honour, and many times it does not. I will say it differently. The honour is always there; it is just delayed. Sometimes the honour is in the age to come, but the honour is always there.

There are seven verbs used in SS2:8-10 to describe the process Jesus uses to awaken us to mature partnership. They include Jesus coming, leaping, skipping, standing, looking, gazing, and speaking. In SS1:4 the Bride prayed, "Draw me and we will run after you". Jesus now introduces the "Let us run" phase of her life. Jesus called her out of the comfort zone so that she might experience deep partnership with Him.

 How responsive are we to the call of God to leave our comfortable world of self-centredness, comfort and safety? To stay behind is to lose a God-given opportunity forever. "Be instant in season and out of season," 2Ti4:2, St Paul advises Timothy. If we obey and follow Him, though difficult, we go to higher levels of fellowship and conformity to Jesus. If we do not follow, it will break fellowship with God.

CONTENTMENT OF SURRENDER

"The voice of my beloved!" SS2:8a. Each time the Bride in the Song of Songs speaks to Jesus she calls Him "my Beloved". When she speaks about Jesus to others, she refers to Him as the One she loves. Each time Jesus speaks to the Bride in the Song, He calls her, "My love", referencing His affection or "fair one", referencing her beauty.

We Groan In Hope 259

"Most assuredly, I say to you, the hour is coming, and now is, when the dead will hear the voice of the Son of God; and those who hear will live. For as the Father has life in Himself, so He has granted the Son to have life in Himself, and has given Him authority to execute judgment also, because He is the Son of Man. Do not marvel at this; for the hour is coming in which all who are in the graves will hear His voice and come forth —those who have done good, to the resurrection of life, and those who have done evil, to the resurrection of condemnation," Jn5:24-29.

The time is now when the dead in sin hear His voice, as the Son of God, and be raised to newness of life, by the power of the Spirit. Then, at the Second coming, the dead in their graves will hear His voice and be raised. There is a "resurrection of life" now and a "resurrection of judgment" then. Those who have indeed passed from spiritual death to life and continued in the light will not come into "judgment". When those who have heard the voice of the Son of God but have not come to the light, who are not of God

nor of the truth, men who have deliberately practiced "evil things" without amendment; when these are called from their tombs, into the presence of Him who executes judgment, it will be to undergo the judgment (2Co5:10).

"The voice of my beloved!" SS2:8a. The words are not those of one dead in trespasses and sins, to whom the Lord is as a root out of a dry ground, without form and comeliness. The speaker has had her eyes opened to behold His beauty, and longs for a fuller enjoyment of His love. "Let Him kiss me with the kisses of His mouth: For Your love is better than wine," SS1:2. It is well that it should be so; it marks a distinct stage in the development of the life of Grace in the soul. And this recorded experience gives, as it were, a Divine warrant for the desire for sensible manifestations of His presence, sensible communications of His love. It was not always so with her. Once she was contented in His absence, other society and other occupations sufficed her; but now it can never be so again. The world can never be to her what it once was; the betrothed Bride has learnt to love her Lord and no other society than His can satisfy her.

We Groan In Hope

 May we believe His testimony; thus, our faith and hope will be in God, and we shall not come into condemnation. And may His voice reach the hearts of those dead in sin; that they may do works meet for repentance, and prepare for the solemn day.

Her Beloved's visits may be occasional and may be brief; He comes and goes but they are precious times of enjoyment. Now her joy in Him is a heaven below; but again, she is longing, and longing in vain, for His presence. Like the ever-changing tide, her experience is an ebbing and flowing one; it may even be that unrest is the rule, satisfaction the exception. Is there no help for this? Must it always continue so? Has He created these unquenchable longings only to tantalize her? Strange indeed it would be if this were the case.

Yet there are many of the Lord's people whose habitual experience corresponds with hers. They do not know the rest, the joy of abiding in Christ; and they do not know how to attain it. There are many who look back to the delightful times of their first espousals, who, so far from finding richer inheritance in Christ than they then had, and are even conscious that they have lost their first love and yet, they might express their experience in the sad lament: Where is the blessedness I knew when first I saw the Lord?

Others, again, who may not have lost their first love, may yet be feeling that the occasional interruptions to communion are becoming more and more unbearable, as the world becomes less and He becomes more. His absence is an ever increasing distress, mistakenly thinking that the Lord has withdrawn the light of His countenance. O, Poor mistaken one! There is a love far stronger than yours waiting, longing for satisfaction. The Bridegroom is waiting for you all the time; the conditions that debar His approach are all of your own making. Take the right place before Him, and He will be most ready, most glad, to satisfy your deepest longings, to meet, supply your every need.

The real secret of an unsatisfied life lies too often in an unsurrendered will. Surrender your own poverty and acknowledge your nothingness to the Lord. Whether you understand it or not, God loves you, is present in you, lives in you, dwells in you, calls you, saves you and offers you an understanding and compassion. There are different levels of surrender, all of which affect our relationship with God. Initial surrender to the drawing of the Holy Spirit leads to salvation (Jn6:44; Acts2:21). When we let go of our own attempts to earn God's favour and rely upon the finished work of Jesus Christ on our behalf, we become a child of God (Jn1:12; 2Co5:21).

But there are times of greater surrender during a Christian's life, which bring deeper intimacy with God and greater power in service. The more areas of our lives we surrender to Him, the more room there is for the filling of the Holy Spirit (Eph5:18). When we are filled with the Holy Spirit, we exhibit traits of His character (Gal 5:22).

Another aspect of surrender to Holy Spirit is a loosening of our hold on certain things. This means we attach less significance and importance to anything and everything. External goals become less and less important and an inner focus on the Heart becomes more and more primary; it becomes our primary source of happiness, of joy, of Grace and ease.

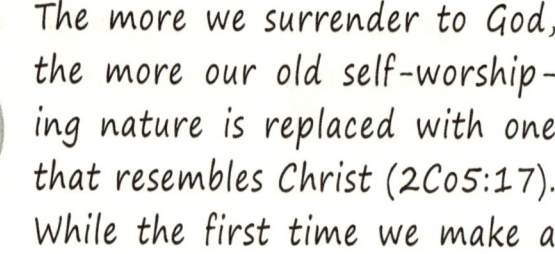 The more we surrender to God, the more our old self-worshiping nature is replaced with one that resembles Christ (2Co5:17). While the first time we make a surrender of our life, thoughts, feelings and heart to Holy Spirit is indeed the most powerful, it is useful and helpful to repeat this act of surrender many times per day.

Our Lord is a wise and beneficent victor; He conquers us to bless us. Do we fancy that we are wiser than He? Or that our love for ourselves is more tender and strong than His? Or that we know ourselves better than He does? How our distrust must grieve and wound afresh the tender heart of Him who was for us the Man of Sorrows! What would be the feelings of an earthly bridegroom if he discovered that his bride-elect was dreading to marry him, lest, when he had the power, he should render her life insupportable? Yet how many of the Lord's redeemed ones treat Him just so! No wonder they are neither happy nor satisfied!

But true love cannot be stationary; it must either decline

or grow. Despite all the unworthy fears of our poor hearts, Divine love is destined to conquer. What should we think of a betrothed one whose conceit and self-will prevented not only the consummation of her own joy, but of his who had given her his heart? Though never at rest in his absence, she cannot trust him fully; and she does not care to give up her own name, her own rights and possessions, her own will to him who has become necessary for her happiness. She would gladly claim him fully, without giving herself fully to him; but it can never be: while she retains her own name, she can never claim his. She may not promise to love and honour if she will not also promise to obey: and till her love reaches that point of surrender she must remain an unsatisfied lover; she cannot, as a satisfied bride, find rest in the home of her husband. While she retains her own will, and the control of her own possessions, she must be content to live on her own resources; she cannot claim His.

Jesus said that His followers must deny themselves (Mk8:34), another call to surrender. The goal of the Christian life can be summed up by Gal 2:20, "I have been crucified with Christ. It is no longer I who live, but Christ lives in me. And the life which I now live in the flesh, I live by faith in the Son of God, who loved me and gave Himself for me." Such a life of surrender is pleasing to God, results in the greatest human fulfilment, and will reap ultimate rewards in heaven (Lk6:22-23). St Paul teaches that God demands that we surrender the totality of our selves; He wants the whole, not a part: "Do not offer any part of yourself to sin as an instrument of wickedness, but rather offer yourselves to God as those who have been brought from death to life; and offer every part of yourself to Him as an instrument of righteousness," Rom6:13.

"Make haste, my Beloved, and be like a gazelle or a young stag on the mountains of spices, SS8:14. The Bride immediately obeys Jesus' exhortation to let Him hear her voice by interceding for Jesus to come quickly. We see the urgency and longing of her heart to be with Jesus. She calls Jesus, "my Beloved" because her love for Him is her strength to the end.

Jesus was revealed as the gazelle and young stag who conquered the mountains in SS2:8, 17. She asks Jesus to come quickly like a swift gazelle and a young stag to conquer all the mountains of opposition and to manifest Himself as the victorious King over all the obstacles of this

We Groan In Hope

age. The Bride offers a threefold prayer that Jesus come near her personally in intimacy, to her city in revival and finally for her at the Second Coming. Her urgent intercession is for Jesus to come quickly.

The Church will "call out" in two directions. First, we will call out to Jesus in intercession to "come to us", and second we will call out to people who thirst to "come to Jesus." We call believers (for revival, discipleship) and unbelievers (by evangelism) to experience the Bridegroom God. The end-time Church has this same prayer. "The Spirit and the Bride say, "Come!" ... "Surely, I am coming quickly," Rev22:17, 20. This will be the first time in history that the Church worldwide will be in dynamic unity with the Spirit. Therefore, the Spirit will be resting on and moving through the Church in great power.

So, Lord Jesus, make haste. Come quickly. Even so, come, Lord Jesus. And until that glorious day, may my garden continually produce its fruit for the delight of Your heart.

www.ingramcontent.com/pod-product-compliance
Lightning Source LLC
Chambersburg PA
CBHW032104090426
42743CB00007B/229